Carrier Lexington

Text and Contemporary Photographs
by HUGH POWER

Introduction by Robert J. Cressman
Foreword by Jerry Chipman

TEXAS A&M UNIVERSITY PRESS
College Station

Library of Congress Cataloging-in-Publication Data

Power, Hugh Irvin, 1947–
  Carrier Lexington / text and contemporary photographs by
Hugh Power ; introduction by Robert J. Cressman ; foreword
by Jerry Chipman. — 1st ed.
    p.   cm. — (Centennial series of the Association of
Former Students, Texas A&M University ; no. 61)
  Includes bibliographical references (p.   ) and index.
  ISBN 0-89096-680-X (cloth, alk. paper)   ISBN 0-89096-681-8
(paper, alk. paper)
    1. Lexington (Aircraft carrier : 1943–1991)—History.
    2. Lexington (Aircraft carrier : 1943–1991)—Pictorial works.
    3. USS Lexington Museum on the Bay (Corpus Christi,
Tex.)—Pictorial works. I. Title. II. Series.
VA65.L4P69   1995
359.9'435'0973—dc20   95-20213
                                                          CIP

TO MY WIFE, BETTY,
who again endured and sustained;
AND TO RUTH HAGAN, INEZ HUGHES,
SELMA BROTZE, AND MARY C. LEA,
those grande dames of the Marshall (Texas)
High School English Department, who
taught that reading well and writing well
are the fountainheads of creativity

Contents

Illustrations

AIRCRAFT

x

Foreword

As the executive director of the USS *Lexington* Museum on the Bay Association, I am proud to offer this foreword to an excellent publishing event. This book documents the development of USS *Lexington* as an aircraft carrier museum. A labor of love by the author, it reflects the same fervor demonstrated by the crew and volunteers who spent thousands of hours nurturing the growth of the steel shell that arrived at Naval Station Ingleside in January of 1992 and turning it into a tribute to U.S. naval aviation history.

The *Lex*'s arrival in the Corpus Christi area in June of 1992 began the guargantuan task of her metamorphosis into a first-class museum. The final berthing of the ship was the result of many months of engineering study, consultation, and ultimate approval of all effected agencies, including the Environmental Protection Agency, Texas Air Control Board, Texas Water Commission, U.S. Army Corps of Engineers, the Governor of Texas, Nueces County, The City of Corpus Christi, the Port Authority, and the U.S. Navy.

Preparations for the ship's arrival required dredging a channel, twelve feet deep and fourteen hundred feet long, from the existing ship channel. When the *Lex* arrived, she was draughting twenty-four feet; allowing for a mean water depth of ten feet and a three-foot tide, this allowed only a one-foot leeway to position the ship before initiating ballasting procedures. Large tugs were used to maintain the ship's position during the first ballasting phase, and even with the unwelcome twenty-five-knot wind out of the southeast, the ship settled into the ditch with the bow almost perfectly on point and the stern thirty feet to starboard of its desired point. The resulting five-degree list to port turned out to be a blessing in disguise, because it created a natural drainage for rainwater. The flight deck, with its expansion joints and many other orifices, made a badly leaking roof over the hangar bay. *Lexington* was immediately filled with 1.5 million gallons of fresh water from two large barges pumping forty-five hundred gallons per minute, which caused the ship to settle on the bottom of the bay. This initial water and the subsequent 4.7 million gallons placed throughout all voids, fourth deck and below, gave the *Lex* a negative ballast of thirty-seven feet. This accumulation of weight will effectively keep the ship in place during a hurricane.

With the final placement of the ship, the development process began; the first order of business was ingress and egress of the ship. Initially, a combination of barges, makeshift saddles, the starboard accommodation ladder, and skiffs from the beach was used. During this phase the 870-foot concrete approachway was constructed, at a cost of $1 million, and safety measures were installed throughout the ship. Over the years, for example, the firemain system had essentially rusted to a state of uselessness, which forced the development of a new system of fire protection. After four months of "field engineering"—which included building a Ship's Store, increasing hangar bay lighting, painting the entire hangar bay and all tour routes, providing signage, and constructing permanent gangways—the ship opened her number three elevator on October 14, 1992, and USS *Lexington* began a new career as a museum dedicated to U.S. naval aviation and its proud history.

To this date, *Lexington*, a nonprofit institution, has received more than one million visitors from all over the world, producing revenues well in excess of operational requirements. This has allowed for continued development of the museum, which now has seventeen different naval aircraft and five distinct tour routes: the Foc'sle; the Admiral's and Captain's Quarters, Combat Information Center (CIC), and Air Operations; the Flight Deck and Bridge; the Hangar Deck; and the Crew's Galley, Sick Bay, and Engine Room.

Lexington is serving other functions in addition to being a naval museum. A youth "live-aboard" program, which has accommodated more than five thousand Boy Scouts, Girl Scouts, and several other youth groups, allows young people to live on the ship for a weekend. The "Science Aboard Ship" educational program is a recent innovation that was developed in concert with several local school districts. Currently focusing on students in the third, fourth, and fifth grades, the program's goal is to develop a hands-on, interactive experience that will satisfy learning objectives of various science classes. The first program taught the workings of simple machines to third-grade students, using examples on the ship to demonstrate levers, fulcrums, wheels and axles, pulleys, and inclined planes.

It is the mission of this ship to be a multi-faceted asset to the community at large. USS *Lexington* not only portrays naval aviation history but also provides a quality experience that contributes to the education, recreation, and well-being of the people of South Texas, the United States, and throughout the world.

—Jerry Chipman
Executive Director,
USS *Lexington*
Museum on the Bay

Preface

No warship has evolved from infancy to sovereignty faster, nor dominated the seas more completely, than the aircraft carrier.

That is perhaps a bold statement and, like similar claims, can be quarreled over. But there is verifiable history to support the aircraft carrier's claim to near-instant dominance, and some of it can be considered here.

It can be fairly stated that no warship type possessed a more questionable pedigree at the outbreak of World War II. The aircraft carrier—in forms unrecognizable today—was on hand for World War I, but its contributions were negligible and restricted by the blinkered vision of those naval commanders whose careers would rise and fall with the big gun. Thus the carrier was an unknown quantity in 1939, for only the carrier among warships lacked a track record.

In contrast, the dreadnought battleship was descended from the great galleys that fought at Actium in 31 B.C. and from Nelson's "wooden walls" of the days of sail, like HMS *Victory*, intact today at the British Royal Navy's Portsmouth yard.

The cruiser could be traced to the nimble sailing frigate, preserved in the United States Navy's *Constitution*. The destroyer had evolved with the torpedo, could trace its ancestry to crude vessels deployed during the American Civil War, and recorded its first successes in the Sino-French War of 1883–85.

As for the submarine, the vision of submersible warships dated to the American Revolution, and only yesterday Germany's U-boats came perilously close to snatching victory in World War I.

That was the way warships were assessed in 1939, when the world's navies deployed sixty-three dreadnoughts and only twenty-five aircraft carriers, a third of which were Japanese. By September, 1945, when Japan surrendered, there remained forty-one dreadnoughts, but the United States alone deployed more than a hundred aircraft carriers of all types and sizes, and

Great Britain had seventy-one. Japan had built and deployed—however briefly—twenty-five carriers and converted two battleships to handle seaplanes. Just four of those survived to surrender.

In only six years, the "unknown quantity" had ended the long reign of the big gun at sea, culminating in the sinking by carrier-based aircraft of the largest battleships ever built, Japan's *Yamato* and *Musashi*. In ever-larger task forces, the carrier had dominated the war in the Pacific and won it for the United States and its allies; had held the "Inland Sea"—the Mediterranean—against both the Italians and Germans; and, in the escort carrier, had been a pivotal player at mastering the submarine in the Atlantic.

There were harbingers of all this, but they were largely ignored. The first unit of the British Grand Fleet to spot the German High Seas Fleet at the Battle of Jutland (May 31, 1916) was not a warship but a seaplane from the carrier *Engadine* (a converted merchantman that had to stop and lower her aircraft in the water with a crane, then stop again and recover them the same way). The plane's message was delayed and played no part in the battle.

In 1921, U.S. Army Gen. Billy Mitchell sank the German dreadnought *Ostfriesland*, a war prize of the United States, with bombs dropped from aircraft. The gun-club admirals dismissed this; the ship was not manned, not under way, and not shooting back. And besides, they argued, Mitchell cheated by using bombs larger than agreed on for the test. Mitchell's planes were land based, and no carriers were involved. But the airplane, like the first clouds of a storm front, had signaled its potential to surface ships of all kinds.

Land targets were next. In 1929, planes from the USS *Saratoga* exposed the vulnerability of the Panama Canal locks to carrier-based attack. And in 1932, *Saratoga* and her sister ship, the first *Lexington* (CV-2), staged a simulated dawn raid on Pearl Harbor with 152 aircraft, less than half the number the Japanese would use in 1941. Pearl Harbor was unprepared and, at least on paper, devastated.

The world's admirals remained blasé. Yet for all their condescension, the world's navies had sought a purpose for the airplane almost as soon as it came into being.

As early as 1910, an aircraft was launched from the bow of the American cruiser *Birmingham*. The Royal Navy had weighed in with an experimental "aircraft-carrier," the converted cruiser HMS *Hermes*, in 1913. That same year, Capt. Murray Sueter of the Royal Navy theorized the mating of the airplane and the torpedo, and a year earlier the fledgling Royal Naval Air Service had conducted the first trials in dropping bombs at sea.

But not until the arrival of purpose-built ships, able to

launch and recover their aircraft while under way, did the realities of air power at sea begin to match the predictions. Ironically, the first true carriers owed their existence to the ship they would eventually displace, the dreadnought.

Meeting in Washington, D.C., in 1921–22 in a desperate effort to derail another arms race, the world's naval powers concluded a treaty that limited the number, size, total tonnage, and gun power of battleships. Those nations with dreadnoughts nearing completion were allowed to finish them as aircraft carriers. Total carrier tonnage was also limited by the Washington Naval Treaty of 1922, though the signatories were probably more worried about re-conversion of the carriers into battleships than about the real potential of aviation at sea.

Thus the first fleet carriers had been laid down as dreadnoughts. *Lexington* and *Saratoga* were converted from what were to be the U.S. Navy's first battlecruisers. Japan converted the battlecruiser *Akagi* and the fast battleship *Kaga*, and Britain rebuilt its hybrid *Furious*- and *Courageous*-class battlecruisers.

In spite of—perhaps because of—such beginnings, the carrier remained a question mark to the admirals, who were unclear about its strategic or tactical uses other than reconnaissance. The carrier still looked more evolutionary than revolutionary. Then, between November of 1940 and June of 1942, the revolution arrived.

It began quietly enough. Through the first year of war in the Atlantic, the carrier claimed only the dubious distinction of being the first capital ship sunk, with HMS *Courageous* falling victim to a U-boat on September 17, 1939.

The Mediterranean was a different story. There the Royal Navy battle line was outgunned and often outnumbered by a modernized Italian navy. But Adm. Andrew Cunningham had, in the carrier *Illustrious*, a card not yet played. On November 11, 1940, he played it with audacity and vigor.

A force of twenty-one Swordfish, an obsolete biplane with a top speed of barely 150 mph and the undistinguished nickname "Stringbag," swept into the Italian fleet anchorage at Taranto in a night attack with torpedoes. When the planes departed, Italy had just two serviceable battleships left, and the naval war in the Mediterranean had been decided, though it would take time to play out.

In May of the following year, the ubiquitous Swordfish struck again, landing the decisive hit in what many regard as the greatest sea chase of all time—the pursuit of the German battleship *Bismarck*. A torpedo launched by a Swordfish from the carrier *Ark Royal* struck *Bismarck*'s rudder and propellers, destroyed her maneuverability and speed, and left her easy prey for the British battleships that finished her off the next day.

Then in December came the Japanese attack on Pearl Harbor, an attack labeled virtually impossible just a week earlier by one veteran American admiral. When the last wave of attackers withdrew, the United States Navy no longer had a battle fleet in the Pacific. Three days later, the Royal Navy was similarly reduced when land-based Japanese aircraft sank the new battleship *Prince of Wales* and the battlecruiser *Repulse*.

These successes would, in the long run, work against the Japanese. With no battleships in the Pacific, the United States turned to its carriers, and the carriers were up to the job.

First in the Coral Sea, where the first *Lexington* was lost, then at Midway, in the most decisive five minutes in U.S. naval history, the aircraft carrier and its planes wrenched the war's momentum from the Japanese. And despite precarious days at Guadalcanal, when *Enterprise* was the only operational U.S. carrier, that momentum was never again lost.

Appearing in 1943, the *Essex*-class carriers made certain of that. This book focuses on one of those ships, the second *Lexington* (CV-16), second ship of her class to commission and one of the most decorated American carriers of the Pacific war. But the book is about all the *Essex*es—about all aircraft carriers, really. It is a book about a sea change in the way we fight on the oceans, the biggest change since sails replaced oars. And *Lexington* has become a laboratory and classroom in which that change can be studied and understood.

No ship could offer more in retirement.

—Hugh Power

Acknowledgments

The preparation of this book has been a family affair.

Defining family is tough, but I think family is as family does, and this family has done two things very well. We have provided each other respect, help, and compassion; and together we have created from ephemeral speculation and concept a work of substantive knowledge and fact.

At this family's core is, once again, the splendid cast and crew of Texas A&M University Press. The Press is a place where I feel at home, and that feeling cannot be bartered for or bought; it must be given willingly, which makes it special.

The staff of the USS *Lexington* Museum on the Bay has been superb. Executive director Jerry Chipman, deputy executive director M. Charles "Rusty" Reustle, former assistant executive director Wayne Fellers, historian Judith Whipple, aircraft maintenance technician John Melita, and every crew member have interrupted their own work to help me. No author can ask for more. Thanks also to the USS *Lexington* Volunteer Organization, which provided a wealth of information for the book's text.

Technical and logistical photographic support was again provided by Jim Cruz, who made the outstanding aerial shots of *Lexington*; Maureen O'Grady, Paula Schuetz, and the familiar crew at Southwestern Camera in Clear Lake, Texas; Diana Carney and Sherri Griffin of Industrial Photographic Supply in Bellaire, Texas; repair specialist Kerry Stamey at Southern Camera Repair in Baton Rouge, Louisiana; and the folks at Houston Camera Repair.

Once more I am grateful for the knowledge, and often the tenacity, taught me by my photography mentors: Bob Burns, former chief photographer of my hometown newspaper, the *Marshall News Messenger*; Smith Kiker at the University of North Texas; and the late—and much missed—Vaden Smith of Galveston.

"Foreign aid" again came from Anthony and Chris

xx

Blackman of Gravesend, England. I drew strength from our correspondence during the creation of *Battleship Texas*, but we had never met. Happily, now we have. Tony and Chris joined me for the *Texas* coming-out party in April, 1993, and both are as marvelous as their letters told me they would be.

Thanks also to J. Bangle and Celia Strain of Bangle Gallery in Galveston for that first book-signing party and for their continued support. Thanks as well to John Powers and his fellow members of the First Naval Corps, Texas Navy, and the Texas Command of the Legion of Frontiersmen of the Commonwealth, for their valued recognition of *Battleship Texas* and for their ongoing support for this volume.

And a big thank-you goes to my real family, "kin," as we say up in northeast Texas. It's a big, warm, enduring clan, and I'm lucky to belong to it. They don't pull their punches, but when you're around them, you're always home. It matters, believe me.

My dedication is self-explanatory, but it is worth saying that my high school English and journalism teachers were forged from a singular mold, and like limited-edition plates, the mold was then broken. I did not know it then, but I was greatly blessed that those women pointed me down the road "less traveled by."

Carrier Lexington

Introduction

Robert J. Cressman

The name *Lexington* evokes the history not only of the United States Navy but of the United States itself, honoring as it does the opening skirmish of the American Revolution in April, 1775, on a village green in Massachusetts. The use of the name by the Continental Navy and then the United States Navy was almost immediate. The lineage of the ship preserved as a memorial in Corpus Christi, Texas, is a long and distinguished one.

The first *Lexington*, a brigantine acquired by the Marine Committee of the Continental Congress on March 13, 1776, had originally been *Wild Duck*. Renamed *Lexington*, the ship sailed under a succession of captains until captured by the British cutter HMS *Alert* on September 19, 1777.

The second *Lexington*, a 24-gun sloop of war built at the New York Navy Yard in 1825, saw service protecting Yankee fishermen off Labrador and "showed the flag" in the Mediterranean and off the west coast of North America. During the conflict with Mexico (1846–48) she transported troops, and she capped off her career by participating in Commodore Matthew Calbraith Perry's expedition to Japan. Decommissioned in 1855, she was sold five years later.

The third *Lexington*, a sidewheel steamer built at Pittsburgh, Pennsylvania, and acquired by the War Department in 1861, was converted to a gunboat at Cincinnati, Ohio. The steamer joined the western flotilla at Cairo, Illinois, on August 12, 1861, and performed significant service during the Civil War on the western rivers. Decommissioned on July 2, 1865, she was sold on August 17, 1865.

The name would not be used again until World War I, when it was originally assigned to a battlecruiser—a ship with the size and armament of a battleship but with the speed and armor of a cruiser. The projected warship was renamed *Ranger*, however, on December 10, 1917, and the name *Lexington* was reassigned to another battlecruiser laid down on January 8, 1921, at Quincy, Massachusetts, by the Fore River Shipbuilding Company. The Washington Treaty on the Limitation of Armaments, signed in February of 1922, however, suspended her construction, and she was completed as an aircraft carrier instead. She and her sister ship *Saratoga* (CV-3) joined *Langley*—the U.S. Navy's first aircraft carrier, converted from a collier—as the U.S. Navy entered the aviation age. The fourth *Lexington*, assigned the hull number CV-2, was commissioned on December 14, 1927.

Unlike battleships, aircraft carriers were not expected to slug it out, toe to toe, with their adversaries. The main battery of the carrier was planes, not the big gun, though *Lexington* and *Saratoga* carried eight-inch guns to deal with enemy cruisers. Some radical naval aviators even believed that aircraft carriers not only could operate independently of battleships but could supplant them.

Lexington served continuously during the 1920s and 1930s, with active service punctuated by periodic overhauls and alterations to increase efficiency and reflect improvements in technology. The carrier planes grew in size as the decades progressed, from biplanes to monoplanes, and *Lexington* participated in yearly exercises that honed the fighting edge of the navy's carrier-based air arm. Fleet exercises took place where tactics were developed, while the air group assigned to *Lexington* carried out a regular schedule of training, both ashore and afloat. The ship gained fame by providing electric power to the city of Tacoma, Washington, in 1930 and by participating in the search for Amelia Earhart after she disappeared during her attempted transpacific flight in July of 1937.

When World War II erupted in Europe in September, 1939, *Lexington* was operating in the Pacific. She was transporting Marine Corps scout bombers to Midway when the Japanese carrier force under Vice Adm. Chuichi Nagumo descended upon the Pacific Fleet at Pearl Harbor on December 7, 1941. The crippling of the battle line propelled the aircraft carrier, screened by cruisers and destroyers, into the forefront of the U.S. Navy's arsenal in the war against Japan.

Lexington participated in the abortive attempt to relieve Wake Island in December, 1941, and acquitted herself well in battle off Bougainville on February 20, 1942, when her combat air patrol (CAP) annihilated a force of Japanese land-based bombers sent out to attack her. She subsequently teamed with *Yorktown* in raiding Japanese ships off Lae and Salamaua, New Guinea, on March 10, 1942, and after a brief modernization overhaul at Pearl Harbor, again joined *Yorktown* to participate in the Battle of the Coral Sea on May 7–8, 1942. This was the first naval battle in history in which neither opponent came within surface gun range of the other. Irreparable bomb and torpedo damage suffered on May 8 necessitated *Lexington*'s destruction by the escorting destroyer *Phelps*.

While the "old" *Lexington* was in active service, the navy had continued to develop a new generation of aircraft carriers that would reflect the operational experience gained in the lineage of ships that began with *Langley*, *Lexington* and *Saratoga*, the one-of-a-kind *Ranger*, and the sister ships *Yorktown* and *Enterprise*. Initially, the designs for the follow-on ships projected carriers similar to those already in service; thus *Wasp* (which followed *Enterprise*) was essentially a redesigned *Ranger*, and *Hornet* (which followed *Wasp*) was a refined duplicate of *Yorktown*.

Congress authorized a new class of carrier, the first of which was named *Essex*, on May 17, 1938; the first ship of that class was ordered on July 19, 1940. Designers projected the *Essex*-class carrier would displace 27,100 tons, based on the ship's being fully loaded except for fuel; would have an 862-by-108-foot flight deck; and would have the capacity to operate four squadrons of planes plus spares. They projected a complement of 2,171, including 632 for the aviation division. Three elevators, one of which would be mounted amidships at the portside edge of the flight deck, would allow faster recovery and spotting of aircraft.

One of the projected *Essex*-class ships had been designated at the outset by the alphanumeric hull number CV-16. In keeping with the then-traditional naming of aircraft carriers for famous former ships, Pres. Franklin D. Roosevelt selected the name *Cabot*—honoring one of the first six Continental Navy warships—for CV-16, which was laid down at Quincy by Bethlehem Steel Company's Fore River yard on July 15, 1941. After workers at Quincy petitioned to honor the memory of the lost *Lexington* (CV-2) by reassigning the name to the new ship, Sec. of the Navy Frank Knox accordingly renamed CV-16 *Lexington* on June 16, 1942.

The fifth *Lexington* was launched September 26, 1942, and christened by Mrs. Theodore Douglas Robinson, who had performed the same honors on the previous ship of the name. Commissioned at the South Boston Navy Yard on February 17, 1943, with Capt. Felix B. Stump in command, *Lexington* fitted-out until April 13, 1943, when she sailed for Hampton Roads. After briefly visiting Annapolis, Maryland, she logged a milestone on April 22 when Cmdr. Bennett W. Wright, the ship's air officer, made the first takeoff and landing in a North American SNJ-4C. Soon thereafter, the new *Lexington*'s "main battery," Air Group (CVG) 16, reported on board. The group included Bombing Squadron (VB) 16, equipped with Douglas SBD-4 Dauntless dive/scout bombers; Fighting Squadron (VF) 16, flying Grumman F4F-4 Wildcat fighters; and Torpedo Squad-

CV-16
BOSTON HARBOR
17 Feb, 1943

Fig. 1. *Lexington,* wearing the Camouflage Measure 21 paint scheme she retained throughout World War II, steams through the ice of Boston Harbor on February 17, 1943, the day she was commissioned. Note the radio antennas on the starboard edge of the flight deck; the pyramidal silhouette of the superstructure, or "island"; the twin 5-inch/38-caliber gun mounts fore and aft of the island; the galleries of Oerlikon 20mm antiaircraft guns on the outboard side of the island; and the partially raised roller curtains at the hangar-deck level. The forward elevator is lowered, and the portside deck-edge elevator is in its stowed, or "up," position. *Courtesy National Archives*

ron (VT) 16, equipped with Grumman TBF-1 Avenger torpedo bombers. By the time the ship was ready to sail for the war zones, VF-16 would be reequipped with the Grumman F6F-3 Hellcat, and VB-16 with the Douglas SBD-5 Dauntless.

After shakedown training out of Trinidad, and repairs and alterations at Boston, *Lexington* sailed on Independence Day of 1943 on the first leg of the voyage to the Pacific theater. Steaming via Norfolk, she reached Cristobal, Canal Zone, where she rendezvoused on July 26 with the light fleet carriers *Belleau Wood* and *Princeton.* After her first transit of the canal, *Lexington* sailed from Balboa on July 28 with a screen of six destroyers.

Fig. 2. Capt. Felix B. Stump, *Lexington*'s first commanding officer. *Courtesy National Archives*

Reaching Hawaiian waters on August 9, *Lexington* conducted several weeks of underway training punctuated by periods of upkeep at the Pearl Harbor Navy Yard. On September 11, 1943, she sailed as flagship of Rear Adm. Charles E. Pownall, Commander, Task Group (TG) 15.5, accompanied by *Belleau Wood* and *Princeton*, three light cruisers, an oiler, and a screen of eight destroyers. A week later, on September 18, *Lexington* launched her first air strikes against Japanese installations on Tarawa, in the Gilbert Islands. These were the prototypes for attacks that fast carrier task forces, supported by a logistics "train" of oilers and supply ships, would carry to the very doorstep of the Japanese home islands.

After a brief respite at Pearl, *Lexington* sailed on September 29, flying the flag of Rear Adm. Arthur W. Radford and accompanied by sister ship *Yorktown* and three light fleet carriers—*Cowpens*, *Independence*, and *Belleau Wood*. *Lexington*'s planes then hit Japanese installations on Wake Island on October 5 and 6.

Lexington sortied again from Pearl on November 10, bound for the Gilbert Islands. Between November 19 and 24, the ship operated with *Yorktown* and *Cowpens*, a hundred miles south-

Fig. 3. Douglas SBD-5 Dauntless dive-bombers of Bombing Squadron (VB) 16 on *Lexington*'s flight deck, September 18, 1943. The planes' standard color scheme at that time was dark blue upper surfaces, feathered on the fuselage into light blue, and white under surfaces. Stars are blue and white, with the entire insignia bordered in red. Individual plane numbers are white. Among the aircraft types operated by *Lexington* during World War II, the Dauntless was the only one without folding wings. *Courtesy National Archives*

east of Mille, in the Marshall Islands, ready to intercept any Japanese planes that attempted to reinforce the Gilberts. From November 19 through November 22, *Lexington*'s planes neutralized Japanese antiaircraft guns and airfields at Mille.

There would be little pause from the onslaught against Japanese bases in the central Pacific. Once the Gilberts had fallen, *Lexington* and her consorts retired to refuel. They then shaped a course for Kwajalein, in the Marshall Islands, along with *Yorktown*, *Cowpens*, four heavy cruisers, a light cruiser, and a screen of destroyers. After the carriers' planes had wreaked havoc on enemy airfields and shipping on December 4, the ship suffered her first battle damage from a Japanese aerial torpedo late that day. Casualties totaled nine dead and thirty-five injured.

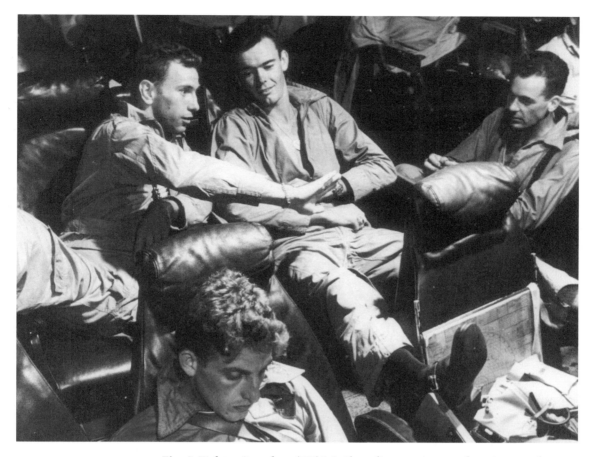

Fig. 4. Fighter Squadron (VF) 16 pilots discuss past combats in one of *Lexington*'s ready rooms. Ens. Edward J. Rucinski, USNR, left, describes how he shot down a Japanese A6M2 Zero fighter, nicknamed "Zeke" by American airmen, by firing at its wingroot tanks on November 23, 1943. Listening attentively are Lt. (j. g.) Eugene R. Hanks, USNR, center, and Lt. (j.g.) Francis M. Fleming, USNR, right. Ens. William J. Seyfferle, USNR, is seated in the foreground. *Courtesy National Archives*

Lexington was drydocked at Pearl Harbor for temporary repairs, transferred CVG-16 ashore, then sailed on December 17 for Bremerton, Washington. The ship reached the Puget Sound Navy Yard three days before Christmas of 1943. Sailing for Alameda on February 12, 1944, she subsequently embarked CVG-19. Passing through the Golden Gate on February 24, she reached Pearl on February 28.

After exchanging CVG-19 for the original air group, CVG-16, *Lexington* sailed for the war zone on March 3, bound for Majuro, in the Marshalls. The ship reached this destination on March 8, when *Lexington* became the flagship for Vice Adm. Marc A. Mitscher, Commander, Task Force (TF) 58. Ten days later, *Lexington*'s planes hit Japanese installations at Mille, and four days after that, she sortied to raid the Palaus. For two days, TF 58 inflicted extensive damage on shipping, aircraft,

10

Fig. 5. Vice Adm. Marc A. Mitscher, seated at far right on the flag bridge of the *Lexington*, listens to reports of the air battles on June 19, 1944. This was the first day of the Battle of the Philippine Sea, where Japan lost so many aircraft that the confrontation became known as the "Marianas Turkey Shoot." *Courtesy National Archives*

and installations; VF-16 carried out masthead bombing attacks while VT-16 sowed mines across the harbor entrance to block the main channel.

The following day, March 23, *Lexington*'s pilots helped demolish Woleai Atoll as a Japanese staging base, but during the recovery of planes that afternoon, a returning Hellcat missed the arresting gear, knocked the wing off another F6F, and crashed into a third. The two locked F6Fs then plunged down into the open number one elevator pit, landing atop a fourth Hellcat, parked on the elevator. The hangar-deck firefighting crew extinguished the blaze, but the pilot of the F6F parked on the elevator, then at hangar-deck level, died instantly in the crash. *Lexington* retired to Majuro, arriving there on April 6.

The next job for TF 58 was supporting the amphibious landings at Hollandia, Dutch New Guinea. This was the first time the fast carriers had been used to help Gen. Douglas MacArthur's southwest Pacific operations. Leaving Majuro on April 13, the task force struck the target on April 21, the day before the troops were scheduled to go ashore. Despite poor

Fig. 6. *Lexington* recovers Grumman F6F-3 Hellcat fighters while under way on March 10, 1944. After recovery by the aft arresting gear, planes taxied forward, where their wings were folded and the aircraft were parked until the recovery cycle was completed. Then flight-deck crew members, their individual duties identified by brightly colored jerseys, would either move the planes aft and position (or "spot") them for the next operation or move them below to the hangar deck. *Courtesy National Archives*

flying weather during the first day's air operations, *Lexington*'s pilots bombed and strafed the Hollandia, Sentani, and Cyclops aerodromes. *Lexington* and her sister ships returned the next morning to continue support for the land operations.

Withdrawn from Hollandia on April 25, TF 58 fueled and then steamed to waters 150 miles north of the objective, ready to render support if needed. Snooping Japanese planes from Guam, Palau, and Biak frequently neared the American ships, and fighters from the CAP downed five. Destroyers *Boyd, Knapp,* and *Dortch* picked up surviving pilots and transported them to *Lexington* for interrogation.

Next on the timetable was Truk, then regarded as Japan's most formidable mid-Pacific base. On the first day of strikes, April 29, *Lexington*'s pilots demolished an ammunition dump, two fuel dumps, and numerous buildings. The next day, her Dauntlesses and Avengers bombed a radio station and a seaplane ramp, among other targets. While the carriers worked over Truk, the heavy cruisers—detached temporarily from the screen—shelled neighboring Satawan Atoll. After ineffective enemy attempts to retaliate, TF 58 retired east toward Ponape, where its fast battleships bombarded Japanese installations.

After several weeks of rest and replenishment at Majuro, *Lexington* sailed on June 6 to assist in the invasion of the Marianas Islands. Inaugurating the attacks on Japanese positions with an afternoon fighter sweep, instead of a dawn attack, paid dividends when *Lexington*'s planes found themselves in uncontested airspace. They strafed Aslito airfield with impunity, destroying what aircraft they found there and contributing to the assumption of control of the skies over Saipan. The planes heavily damaged installations and facilities in the target area, as well as two cargo vessels and numerous small craft. The following day, the planes hit Garapan Town; fires dotting the target area testified to the extent of damage inflicted. On June 14, *Lexington* and the other TF 58 carriers hit enemy installations on islands north of Saipan and on Saipan itself. Her planes then flew close support for the landings.

Late that day, during recovery of the last strike, *Lexington*'s radar picked up an increasing number of incoming "bogeys." The crew hastened to battle stations while the ship continued to recover her planes. The bogeys multiplied until the radar screen showed five raids in progress at the same time. The CAP from light fleet carrier *San Jacinto* shot down six "Tonys" (Kawasaki Ki-61 Army Type 3 fighters) thirty miles out. Moments later, *Lexington*'s lookouts spotted ten twin-engined bombers dead ahead and closing fast.

Despite heavy antiaircraft fire, the Japanese planes determinedly charged through it. *Lexington*'s guns opened fire at eight of the planes plainly visible off the port and starboard bows, and with supporting fire from screening ships, splashed five in quick succession. *Lexington* then passed between the tracks of two torpedoes whose courses paralleled the ship's. Another attacker burst into flames off the starboard bow but remained airborne, passed diagonally a few feet above the flight deck, and then crashed into the sea on the port quarter.

On June 16, *Lexington* launched one close support strike while the task group maneuvered and fueled. "Scuttlebutt" had it that the Japanese fleet had decided to challenge the American fleet supporting the occupation of Saipan, a rumor in part confirmed by the gathering of TF 58's fast battleships into a special strike force. *Lexington*'s planes flew a special strike against targets on Guam, as well as routine patrols. Her radar picked up two bogeys that night, and although the ship went to general quarters, nothing ensued. As the task force

Fig. 7. *Lexington* is seen from the rear cockpit of a just-launched Dauntless dive-bomber on June 13, 1944, shortly before the Battle of the Philippine Sea. Note the forest of radar antennas adorning the island and the radio antennas at the edge of the flight deck, which have been rotated to a horizontal position to avoid interfering with flight operations. *Courtesy National Archives*

steamed west of the Marianas on June 17, searching for the Japanese fleet, the CAP shot down several "snoopers." None of the American long-range searches disclosed any enemy activity.

June 19 dawned with the exact whereabouts of the Japanese a mystery, although an unusually large number of single bogey interceptions hinted at the Japanese presence somewhere between TF 58 and the Philippines. During the early morning, *Belleau Wood*'s planes noted that many Japanese aircraft were landing on the island. *Lexington* launched a division of her own fighters to assist *Belleau Wood*.

Soon thereafter, radar disclosed a very large group of bogeys approaching from the west. *Lexington* spotted her deck

Fig. 8. A General Motors–built TBM-1D Avenger torpedo bomber, identifiable by the radome on the leading edge of the wing, is centered among several Grumman-built TBF-1 Avengers spotted forward on *Lexington*'s flight deck on June 15, 1944. The Avenger could deliver either torpedoes or bombs, and it did both in the Pacific. Parked among the Avengers are several Dauntless dive-bombers, identifiable by their non-folding wings and perforated dive brakes. *Courtesy National Archives*

for a strike; ordnance-laden bombers and torpedo planes lumbered aloft, and all fighters were scrambled. Admiral Mitscher ordered all planes to drop their bombs on Guam.

The ensuing Battle of the Philippine Sea found CVG-16 in the thick of the fight, as TF 58's planes and gunfire destroyed more than three hundred Japanese planes in the first day's action—which would come to be known as the Marianas Turkey Shoot. Submarines *Cavalla* and *Albacore* contributed to the victory by sinking the Japanese carriers *Shokaku* and *Taiho*, respectively. *Lexington* planes shot down straggling enemy aircraft attempting to reach Guam.

The next day, June 20, the search continued for straggling Japanese surface units; at mid-afternoon, a plane from another

Fig. 9. With two *Lexington* seamen smiling approval, Lt. (j.g.) Alexander Vraciu of Fighter Squadron (VF) 16 holds up six fingers, one for each of the Yokosuka D4Y "Judy" dive-bombers he shot down on June 19, 1944, the first day of the Marianas Turkey Shoot. Behind Vraciu is an F6F-3 Hellcat fighter. *Courtesy National Archives*

task group spotted enemy ships. Despite the late hour and the long range, Admiral Mitscher elected to launch a strike to which *Lexington* contributed eleven Hellcats, seven Avengers, and fifteen Dauntlesses. The American strike force found the Japanese and in the melee sank the light carrier *Hiyo* and inflicted damage on three other carriers, a battleship, a heavy cruiser, and a fleet oiler. Two other Japanese auxiliary vessels suffered damage severe enough to force them to scuttle.

The first planes began returning well after sunset; Mitscher, accepting the risk, ordered the ships to turn on their lights to aid recovery operations in the gathering darkness. Eventually, *Lexington* recovered twenty-two of her own air group and twelve from other carriers. A total of fourteen *Lexington* planes found a safe haven on board other carriers. Three had been shot down over the Japanese ships, while one Hellcat, one Dauntless, and two Avengers ditched in sight of the task force, where three destroyers and a light cruiser rescued their crews.

Floatplanes from two cruisers rescued the crew of a *Lexington* plane that had been shot down in the vicinity of the enemy fleet.

The one strike launched the next day encountered no enemy ships—the Japanese had withdrawn out of reach during the night—and the task force spent the remainder of the day sorting out which pilots, aircrew, and planes belonged on board which ship. Retiring toward Saipan, the task groups fueled in preparation for the next operation. The two-day Battle of the Philippine Sea cost the Imperial Japanese Navy heavily in terms of pilots and planes, neither of which could be easily replaced.

Remaining in the Marianas between June 25 and July 5, *Lexington* conducted "milk runs" to deny the Japanese use of the airfields on Guam, balancing the combat missions with routine patrols as CVG-16 wound up its tour on board. Considerable night fighter activity enlivened life for the ship during that time, as Japanese snoopers prowled the area each evening between Palau and Truk. *Lexington* headed for Eniwetok on July 6, and on the morning of July 9 launched CVG-16 for the last time.

Lexington—with CVG-19 on board and with its bombing squadron equipped with new Curtiss SB2C Helldivers—sortied from Eniwetok on July 14 and headed for the Marianas. From July 18 through July 21, her planes flew support for landings on Guam, a task made easier by the previous destruction of enemy air power during the capture of Saipan. Ten days later, after fueling, *Lexington* left the Marianas, bound for Palau. There her pilots carried out three days of air strikes on Japanese positions before the ship retired toward the Marianas once more to refuel and rearm, anchoring at Saipan on July 31.

After replenishment, *Lexington* sailed for the Bonin Islands, carrying out strikes against Iwo Jima, Haha Jima, and Chichi Jima. CVG-19 carried out its operations smoothly in spite of poor weather conditions. Upon completion of those operations, *Lexington* returned to Eniwetok on August 10. She remained there until August 29.

During September 6–8, *Lexington*'s pilots struck Palau, destroying enemy defenses prior to invasion and marking the last time the ship would participate in assaults on the outlying perimeter of the Japanese empire. On September 9–10, *Lexington*'s pilots concentrated on installations on Mindanao, in the Philippines. Admiral Halsey's Third Fleet then swung north, and the fast carriers hit the Visayan Islands against stiff Japanese fighter opposition.

Lexington pilots bombed and strafed the Visayans for three days, and with the exception of a solitary bogey that dropped a bomb near *Lexington*, enemy planes did not attack the task force. With support of the Palau landings handled by the escort carriers, the fast fleet carriers pounded north and carried out the first of many strikes against Japanese targets near Manila, the Philippine capital.

On September 21, *Lexington* hurled four strikes against planes on the ground, as well as hangars, other installations, and two coastal convoys steaming up the west side of Luzon. Bogeys closed the formation the next morning, and *Lexington* put her first strike aloft despite the disconcerting accompaniment of gunfire from her own batteries. As she retired from the Philippines, her Helldivers and Hellcats hit enemy shipping in Coron Bay, reportedly a concentration point for Japanese convoys.

The fast carrier task groups then split up and retired toward various atolls and island bases for rest and recreation. While some drew Saipan and Manus, *Lexington* and her consorts ended up at Kossel Roads, then Ulithi, in the Caroline Islands.

On October 6, *Lexington* sailed for a series of operations that eventually led to Japan proper. On October 10, her planes hit Japanese aircraft and shipping in the Nansei Shoto Islands. *Lexington* and the rest of TG 38.2 then pressed on for Formosa. En route, on October 11, *Lexington*'s radar picked up "many bogeys" low on the water, twenty-six miles out and closing. CAP fighters splashed at least six, and ships' gunfire five. Over the next two hours, four or five Japanese "hecklers" encountered intermittent antiaircraft fire near the task force. During the remainder of the night and into the early morning, thirty to forty enemy planes closed the formation to draw fire at least six or seven times, and flares occasionally pierced the darkness.

Lexington's crew remained at general quarters as October 13 dawned and revealed once more the presence of hecklers. After a period in which *Lexington* made smoke, dawn flight operations went as scheduled, and the planes hit their targets as planned. Late that afternoon, however, a report from a *Belleau Wood* plane indicated that the enemy was apparently moving planes in from bases on Luzon to attack the force. At dusk, a Japanese plane torpedoed the heavy cruiser *Canberra*; three light cruisers and four destroyers were detached to lend a hand. *Lexington* helped provide cover for the retirement of the damaged cruiser by launching strikes against Formosa. In the waning daylight, one enemy plane crashed into light cruiser *Reno*'s fantail, and another torpedoed the light cruiser *Houston*. Intermittent attacks continued throughout the night.

After fueling, *Lexington* spent several days steaming in wait for Japanese fleet units reportedly on the move. The ship also dispatched covering planes to protect the damaged cruisers *Canberra* and *Houston* as they doggedly plodded out of the battle area under tow. On October 21, *Lexington* planes flew ninety sorties against Japanese installations on southern Luzon and in the Visayans, including a long-range fighter sweep to Coron Island.

The ship then stood by for three days, until receiving orders to steam toward Luzon and carry out a series of strikes on October 24. *Lexington*'s group was the only one assigned to Luzon; the others to the south were attacking the Visayans and guarding the entrance to San Bernardino Strait. Since prowling submarines had reported Japanese fleet units approaching the Philippines from the west, *Lexington* and her consorts drew the duty of searching an area, three hundred miles wide, to the west of Luzon. While other planes from the task group were to strike Manila, *Lexington* launched five teams, of four fighters and four dive-bombers each, to carry out the required search.

At 0800, radar plot reported the presence of "many bogeys," and *Lexington* scrambled all available fighters to intercept the incoming raid. Persistent air attacks followed, coming from Luzon and from the northeast, with an estimated two hundred planes taking part. Fighters splashed or turned back all but a few of the attackers, while the task group maneuvered into a sheltering rain squall. One of the few enemy planes that succeeded in penetrating the defenses, however, scored a direct hit on *Princeton* at mid-morning, triggering fires and explosions that eventually led to her destruction.

As it became evident that Japanese carriers were steaming northward, *Lexington* and the other carriers launched every available plane to strike the enemy, even while the massive enemy attack was in progress. *Lexington*'s pilots and aircrew pressed home attacks on the Japanese fleet, obtaining hits on a battleship and three cruisers.

Japanese planes appeared over the task group again at 1500, even while searches scoured the waters to the north to locate the enemy carriers. The fighters scrambled from *Lexington* intercepted and broke up the attack, although one group of bogeys penetrated the CAP and got close enough to *Lexington* to drop a bomb off the ship's starboard quarter. In an hour's time, the attack appeared to be over. Despite the bad weather, task force CAP fighters had splashed an estimated 100 to 125 planes; search planes downed another 50 to 60. *Lexington*'s CAP claimed at least 28 of those, and her search planes claimed a further 33.

More action was to come. American search planes located two Japanese task groups, one of which included carriers. That was Vice Adm. Jisaburo Ozawa's decoy force, sent to draw Halsey's carriers away from Vice Adm. Takeo Kurita's battleships and cruisers. Because the strike planes that had flown against the Japanese surface force in the Sibuyan Sea had not yet returned, and because of the distance involved, it was not considered advisable to attack the new force that had been spotted on October 24. That would have to wait until the next day. One of the forces spotted by the search planes included a battleship and what appeared to be four to six cruisers and six destroyers. The other force included the carriers *Zuikaku*, *Zuiho*, *Chiyoda*, and *Chitose*.

Night search planes fixed the location of the Japanese forces again the following morning, and *Lexington*, whose task group had joined the other two in the Third Fleet, launched dawn strikes. While the strike groups orbited the task force, search planes from the American carriers sighted the enemy ships 130 miles away; strikes were soon vectored to the target. The Japanese flattops had flown the bulk of their remaining planes to Luzon after the engagement of the day before, leaving only thirteen aircraft to protect virtually all that remained of the Japanese navy's once powerful carrier arm.

The Hellcats easily overcame that meager fighter opposition, and TF 58's planes sank *Zuikaku*, *Zuiho*, and *Chitose* and crippled *Chiyoda*, which was later sunk by surface gunfire. This virtually eliminated what had once been the world's most powerful naval air arm. For the next two days, *Lexington* steamed east of the Visayans before returning to Ulithi to replenish and rearm.

The respite was brief, and *Lexington* returned to the Visayans again November 1, as a prelude to strikes on Luzon on November 5–6, against enemy shipping, planes, and aircraft facilities. *Lexington* planes pounded Clark Field and applied the coup de grâce to the heavy cruiser *Nachi* in Manila Bay.

But *Lexington* was about to meet a new foe, the kamikaze ("divine wind"). At about 1300 on November 5, *Lexington* detected enemy planes eighty to ninety miles to the west, and scrambled fighters to intercept. Four successive CAPs from her own task group, and two from others nearby, attempted to intercept the inbound strike, which consisted of about seven planes. The CAP managed to splash only one intruder, however, and the heavy cloud cover allowed the rest to attack TG 38.3. At 1338, *Lexington*'s guns splashed a "Zeke" (Mitsubishi A6M5 Navy Type 0 carrier fighter—the latest model of the famed Zero) a thousand yards off the starboard beam.

Soon thereafter, lookouts spotted a second "Zeke" pressing home a similar attack. Despite the heavy antiaircraft barrage, the Japanese pilot dropped his ordnance and followed it into the after starboard side of the island structure. The bomb exploded against the armor plate of Battle II, shattering it and demolishing all of the secondary conning station and its communications equipment. *Lexington*'s guns, meanwhile, shot down another "Zeke" attempting to crash the nearby *Ticonderoga*.

The kamikaze had disintegrated upon impact with the island structure. Fragments and burning gasoline, along with the effect of bomb blast and fragmentation, caused many casualties and serious damage to the signal bridge as well as several 20mm and 40mm batteries. Damage control parties controlled the blaze within twenty minutes, but 42 men died instantly, and a further 8 were listed as missing. Some 132 men had been injured. Fortunately, with the damage confined to the island, *Lexington*'s flight deck had not been touched, permitting the ship to recover the strike groups that had been aloft when the suicide plane hit.

Lexington carried out strikes against targets on Luzon the following day, November 6, then set course for Ulithi, where she transferred her wounded to the hospital ship *Solace* upon arrival on November 9. *Lexington* received the repair ship *Jason* alongside on November 10.

While *Lexington* underwent repairs for battle damage, CVG-20 replaced CVG-19, which was bound for a rest stateside. *Lexington*'s new air group, however, differed markedly from what the ship's air department had been accustomed to: CVG-20 brought on board seventy-three fighters and only fifteen torpedo planes and fifteen bombers.

After a brief working-up period with the new air group, conducted out of Ulithi, *Lexington* sortied on December 11, 1944. As flagship for Rear Adm. Gerald F. Bogan, she was assigned the task of neutralizing enemy air power and denying the Japanese the use of the harbor facilities of Luzon, in support of the occupation of the island of Mindoro. CVG-20 drew the specific task of attacking Clark, Mabalacat, and Bamban airfields.

At 0630 on December 14, *Lexington* launched two fighter sweeps, one with sixteen fighters and a second with fourteen fighters and two camera-equipped photo planes. As the first formed up in the bad weather, flying on instruments, two Hellcats collided in midair, damaging one so badly that the pilot bailed out. A destroyer recovered him a day later. The second plane made it back to *Lexington* and landed without further incident. Upon reaching the target area, the first sweep shot down four of the six Japanese planes attempting to get aloft from one of Clark's runways and burned three planes on the ground in strafing and rocket attacks. Covered by the planes from the first sweep, the second shot down two "Tojos" (Nakajima Ki-44, Army Type 2 single-seat fighter) and a "Betty" (Mitsubishi G4M Navy Type 1 land attack plane) at the cost of one Hellcat, whose pilot was picked up by a destroyer the next day.

A third sweep relieved the second over Clark Field and encountered no air opposition, strafing grounded planes at Clark and Bamban and bombing and rocketing antiaircraft positions and revetments. Despite the intense antiaircraft fire over the target, all planes returned safely. A fourth sweep of ten fight-

Fig. 10. *Lexington*, in the upper left background, stands out in her dark blue paint scheme among other *Essex*-class carriers in this often-published "Murderer's Row" photograph, taken in the anchorage at Ulithi Atoll on December 8, 1944. The other carriers are wearing three-tone Measure 32 "Disruptive" camouflage paint schemes. *Courtesy National Archives*

ers and two camera planes encountered no enemy planes but lost three planes to the "intense and accurate" antiaircraft fire. Only one of these pilots survived and was rescued by Filipino guerrillas.

A fifth sweep hit Clark Field and encountered no air opposition but ran into heavy antiaircraft fire that downed two Hellcats. One pilot was killed, and the other bailed out and landed safely in the hands of Filipino guerrillas.

On December 15 and 16, *Lexington*'s planes again returned to pound the airfields on Luzon, this time with the Helldivers from VB-20 and Avengers from VT-20 taking part. The strikes followed a familiar pattern, with no air interception but with heavy antiaircraft fire. Strike ordnance varied from the standard bombs and rockets to 350-pound depth charges. The strikes destroyed fewer planes on the ground than previous raids had, because the attackers devoted their chief efforts to knocking out the troublesome antiaircraft guns. On December 15, enemy ground fire damaged a Helldiver, forcing the wounded pilot to make a water landing between the east coast of Luzon and the task force. A Kingfisher from one of the screening cruisers sped to the scene, but the pilot had died in the interim. The floatplane rescued the radio operator/gunner, however, and returned him to the task force in good condition. Antiaircraft fire claimed a second SB2C on December 16, but observers saw both the pilot and radio operator/gunner bail out; the latter, picked up by Filipino guerrillas, helped them in their fight against their occupiers.

As almost a footnote to the three days of intense strikes aimed at the airfields of Luzon, two "Bettys", two "Oscars" (Nakajima Ki-43 Army Type 1 fighters), and four "Zeke"s departed the coastline and headed in the direction of the task force. Planes from *Hancock* spotted them near Baler Point, Luzon, and attacked. Planes from *Lexington*, then en route to the target, heard the "tallyho," turned back, and shot down five of the attackers. *Hancock*'s planes shot down both "Bettys" and one of the escorts.

Soon after, on December 19, *Lexington*'s sailors battled a different enemy—the weather—as the fleet found itself in the center of a typhoon east of the Philippines. Three destroyers capsized in the tempest, and although four light fleet carriers, four escort carriers, a light cruiser, seven destroyers, three destroyer escorts, an oiler, and a fleet tug suffered damage, *Lexington* and her sister ships weathered the typhoon.

On December 23, *Lexington* reached Ulithi ("that well-known resort," one *Lexington* crew member described it), where she remained over the Christmas holiday. Under way again on December 30, *Lexington* sailed as Admiral Bogan's flagship (TG 38.2). For the next three weeks, she participated in neutralizing Japanese air and naval power from Nansei Shoto to Luzon and from Indochina to Hong Kong and Okinawa, all part of the unfolding support for the landings at Lingayen Gulf, Luzon.

To that end, CVG-20 conducted strikes on aircraft, aircraft installations, and shipping in the vicinity of southern Formosa January 3 and 4, 1945. Adverse weather over the island and to the east of it hindered the attacks and compelled the pilots to fly on instruments a great deal of the time. With the airfields effectively closed down—permitting the destruction of only five planes—CVG-20 hunted shipping to the west of Formosa, where better weather prevailed. Heavy concentrations of ships in harbor at Takao and Tohsien were located, as was a small convoy fifteen miles west of Formosa. VF-20 Hellcats damaged six ships, assisted in sinking one, and probably sank an escort vessel. They also splashed four enemy fighters. On January 4, though, antiaircraft fire shot down an Avenger. The crew survived, but the subsequent attempt to recover the men by submarine was unsuccessful.

On January 6 and 7, CVG-20 returned to Clark Field and

northern Luzon. Battling foul weather, *Lexington*'s pilots destroyed one Japanese plane in the air and four on the ground, damaged eight planes on the ground, and damaged two ships. Unusually heavy air opposition downed one Hellcat whose pilot survived a harrowing ditching experience.

Lexington's planes resumed strikes on southern Formosa on January 9, sinking or damaging several patrol craft and coastal freighters before the task group steamed into the South China Sea. Three days later, *Lexington* launched the first strikes on shipping and installations along the coast of French Indochina.

After a search disclosed no ships at Nha-trang, a fighter sweep from *Lexington* spotted three Japanese escort vessels in a small bay south of Cape Varella, with Hellcats from *Hancock* and *Hornet* circling and preparing for a strafing run. Due to a communications mix-up, Hellcats from both *Hornet* and *Lexington* simultaneously converged on the targets, and stray .50-caliber rounds compelled one VF-20 pilot to ditch his plane at sea, where a lifeguard submarine rescued him. VF-20 Hellcats, meanwhile, eventually broke off their strafing runs and headed north, where they spotted a small convoy a mile off Qui-nhon, plodding northward at six knots. After sending off a contact report, *Lexington*'s fighters destroyed three "Jakes" (Aichi E13A1 Navy Type 00 reconnaissance floatplanes) and a "Mavis" (Kawanishi H6K5 Navy Type 97 flying boat) at the seaplane base at Qui-nhon.

Lexington launched fifteen Hellcats, twelve of which carried five hundred-pound bombs; eight Avengers; and six Helldivers at noon to attack the convoy that the earlier sweep had disclosed that morning. Flying to the target through very bad weather—the ceiling was about five hundred feet—and joining up with planes from *Hornet* and *Hancock* en route, *Lexington*'s group made contact soon after and attacked. The Avengers attacked the convoy flagship–the light cruiser *Kashii*—and made their runs from seaward. Each of the three torpedo-carrying Avengers obtained hits, all of the "fish" striking amidships or aft. Heavy antiaircraft fire, however, splashed one Avenger.

The rest of the Avengers, carrying five hundred-pounders, glide-bombed *Kashii*, scoring direct hits amidships and on the fantail, and either a direct hit or a near miss off her bow. Four Hellcats also attacked the hapless cruiser and scored at least two direct hits. *Kashii*'s gunners, however, shot down an F6F that plunged straight into the water off the cruiser's stern.

By the end of the day, *Lexington*'s planes had teamed with those from *Hornet* and *Hancock* to sink *Kashii*, two escort vessels, six freighters, and two tankers and to inflict minor damage on three escort vessels. A later strike directed toward the shipping north of Qui-nhon found that the convoy had already been heavily damaged by the time it reached the scene. Air opposition to a strike over Saigon prompted the diversion of eight Hellcats that strafed the airfield at Bien-hoa and bombed revetted aircraft and what appeared to be a barracks.

Over the next several days, *Lexington*'s planes ranged from the Pescadores to Hong Kong. On January 15, they attacked shipping off the former, leaving an old destroyer in sinking condition. The following day, VF-20 F6Fs participated in a series of sweeps on airfields, shipping, and harbor installations at Hong Kong and Kowloon. Although the intense antiaircraft fire shot down no *Lexington* planes, one of her search teams (one SB2C and two F6Fs) found itself set upon by six "Zekes" off Hainan Island, and the SB2C and one F6F were shot down. A lifeguard submarine rescued the fighter pilot.

Lexington passed through the Luzon Straits on the night of January 20, standing toward Formosa. Favorable weather permitted large-scale attacks on airstrips on Formosa, but the Japanese had dispersed their planes and camouflaged them well, making the job of destroying them more difficult. Pilots returning the next day reported only ten planes destroyed and six damaged. Shipping in Toshien and Takao harbors was again battered by *Lexington*'s planes, as were hangars and other installations. During the attack on Toshien, antiaircraft fire splashed an SB2C, killing its crew, and a Hellcat. The latter ditched twelve miles south of Takao, where a lifeguard submarine rescued the pilot.

After *Lexington*'s planes struck Japanese installations on Okinawa on January 22, the ship retired to Ulithi, reaching her destination on January 27. Soon thereafter, Rear Adm. Ralph E. Davison raised his flag on the carrier and relieved Admiral Bogan.

Soon thereafter, on February 2, CVG-9 relieved CVG-20. Eight days later, *Lexington* weighed anchor and sailed for the heartland of the Japanese empire. There was no time for the ship's new air group to enjoy a working-up period; its first mission would be one aimed at the area surrounding Tokyo.

The new operation saw the return of Adm. Raymond A. Spruance as commander of the Fifth Fleet, and Admiral Mitscher as commander of TF 58. Leaving Ulithi, TF 58 steamed east of Saipan and then swung north, as search planes and destroyers swept ahead of the force to destroy any picketboats the enemy had stationed in those waters. For the strikes slated to begin on February 16, the target area lay to the east and southeast of Tokyo, encompassing all of the Chiba Peninsula except the southern tip. In that area lay fifteen airfields and a seaplane base, with the most important at Kisarazu, Natori, and Mobara.

On the morning of February 16, *Lexington* launched a fighter sweep that sped to the target beneath a cloak of clouds,

Fig. 11. Curtiss SB2C-3 Helldiver dive-bombers from Bombing Squadron (VB) 9 are shown after leaving *Lexington*, at lower center, en route to attack the Nakajima Oka aircraft plant forty-five miles northwest of Tokyo on February 16, 1945. Steaming in the distance are, at left, an *Independence*-class light fleet carrier and, right, a *New Orleans*–class heavy cruiser. *Courtesy National Archives*

rain squalls, and a low ceiling off the coast of Honshu. CVG-9's fighters hammered the fighter airstrip at Katori, carrying out their initial strafing passes on what appeared to be at least seventy planes on the ground. Leaving at least eight destroyed aircraft behind them, *Lexington*'s fighters then shot down thirteen Japanese planes without any loss themselves. As the day progressed, however, enemy air and antiaircraft opposition intensified over the Chiba Peninsula and the airfields to the north.

Lexington later sent a strike of sixteen fighters, thirteen bombers, and fifteen bomb-carrying TBMs to destroy an airframe assembly factory northwest of Tokyo. Meanwhile, *Lexington* remained at general quarters until 1915; the ship sounded torpedo defense quarters twice, but no enemy planes approached closer than fifteen miles.

On February 17, the second anniversary of *Lexington*'s commissioning, the carrier sent two sweeps of fighters at targets near Tokyo. After finding Kizarazu "socked in," the first sweep turned its attention to Mobara, east of the enemy capital, where it shot down three "Zekes" and an "Oscar" and probably destroyed a fifth plane on the ground. The second sweep, covering a *Hancock* strike, saw twenty-five or thirty enemy planes retire toward Tokyo, but bad weather over the target resulted in a cancellation of further operations.

Lexington and her consorts then steamed toward Iwo Jima, where she and her sister ships provided close air support attacks against Japanese gun positions on February 19, 21, and 22. On February 22, the pilots experienced frustration when probably half of the napalm-filled belly tanks dropped on Japanese emplacements failed to ignite. During this time, *Lexington* engaged in an underway rearming from the ammunition ship *Shasta*.

On February 23, TF 58 moved northward, and two days later *Lexington* put aloft two fighter sweeps and one deck-load strike earmarked for targets in the vicinity of Tokyo. Encountering no air opposition, her planes destroyed one aircraft, probably destroyed another, and damaged five at snow-covered Tsukuba field, well to the north of the target area. Finding the assigned targets south of Tokyo cloaked in bad weather, the strike planes jettisoned their bombs and returned to the ship. Continued bad weather nullified further attempts at conducting strikes as TF 58 moved westward, until the weather cleared as the force neared the Nansei Shoto chain. Because the two airfields there presented few opportunities for inflicting damage, *Lexington*'s pilots went after shipping instead, damaging eleven ships in addition to luggers and small craft. In the wake of that attack, *Lexington* retired to Ulithi, arriving there March 5.

During the operations against Japan, CVG-9 had destroyed thirty-four planes in the air and twenty-one on the ground, against the loss of five in combat and eleven operationally (seven of these were jettisoned over the side when they were deemed irreparable). In addition to demonstrating the feasibility of operating with near impunity in the waters near Japan, *Lexington* and the fast carrier task force had shown that cold-weather operations, in encountering temperatures as low as forty-one degrees, could be undertaken without any loss of operating efficiency. *Lexington* did not come under attack from any enemy planes during the entire period, although she did fire thirty-eight rounds of radar-controlled five-inch at a Japanese plane five miles away on the night of February 21 off Iwo Jima.

On March 5, *Lexington*, now slated to return to the United States for overhaul, dropped anchor at Ulithi, and Admiral Davison hauled down his flag and departed the ship with his staff. On the following day CVG-9 disembarked, its place taken by CVG-3 for the trip stateside. On March 7, *Lexington* sailed for home. Proceeding via Pearl Harbor, she would up her home-

Fig. 12. Pilots and enlisted men of Fighter-Bomber Squadron (VBF) 94 pose in front of a Vought F4U-4 Corsair aboard *Lexington* during the ship's third war cruise, which began in June of 1945. This was the only war cruise during which the ship operated the famous "Bent-Wing Bird," though Corsairs were aboard as part of Air Group (CVG) 92's aircraft complement during the immediate postwar period. *Courtesy Naval Historical Center*

ward voyage on March 27 at Puget Sound and entered the navy yard four days later.

Lexington completed her navy yard availability period on May 12 but was unable to develop full power during post-overhaul trials, and she returned briefly to the yard for adjustments. Concluding her readiness-for-sea period on May 22, she cleared Seattle that same day. After pausing briefly at Alameda, California, *Lexington* got under way for Pearl Harbor on May 29.

Reaching the destination on June 4, *Lexington* reported for temporary operational control to ComCarDiv 11 the following day, and embarked CVG-94, which was equipped with Hellcats, Corsairs, Helldivers, and Avengers. Between June 6 and 11, *Lexington* trained in Hawaiian waters, when she briefly operated CVG-2 in place of CVG-94 (June 9–10). CVG-94 returned to the ship on June 10.

Under way from Pearl on June 13, *Lexington*, along with *Hancock*, *Cowpens*, and a screen of five destroyers, subsequently raided Wake Island on June 20 to provide combat training for the embarked air groups. Continuing to the Philippines, *Lexington* entered Leyte Gulf six days later. After voyage repairs and replenishment, *Lexington* got under way on July 1, bound once more for Japan. On July 10, CVG-94 began a series of low-level strikes against seven airfields in the vicinity of Tokyo, the most southerly of which were located sixty miles north of the enemy capital.

Steaming next to Hokkaido, *Lexington* found abysmal weather and cancelled the strikes planned for July 13. While bad weather prevented pilots from hitting the assigned airstrips on the northern coastline, *Lexington*'s aviators found many targets, particularly near Koshiro, to the south and east. While battleships and cruisers detached from the task force bombarded the ironworks at Kamaishi, *Lexington* planes flew supporting CAP and photographic missions.

TF 38 pounded targets on Hokkaido again on July 15 and on July 17 and 18 hit the airfields north of Tokyo. On July 18, *Lexington*'s planes joined in the large-scale attack that further damaged the battleship *Nagato* at Yokosuka. After several days of rest, rearming, replenishment, and fueling, *Lexington* and her sister ships resumed strikes on Hamamatsu and four other airfield targets assigned to her, in addition to remnants of the Japanese fleet at Kure.

On July 25, *Lexington*'s planes hit airfields southeast of Nagoya and the naval base at Kure. After fueling and rearming on two following days, *Lexington* carried out operations against Nagoya on July 28 and 30. Bad weather compelled the cancellation of strikes against Kyushu.

On August 6, the first atomic bomb was dropped from a Boeing B-29 Superfortress, destroying the city of Hiroshima. Word of that event reached *Lexington*, steaming northward some three hundred miles off Honshu. A second atomic bomb destroyed Nagasaki three days later, the same day that CVG-94 hit northern Honshu. Retiring on the evening of August 10, *Lexington* resumed offensive operations three days later with an attack against the Tokyo-Shibura works at Kawasaki, and then strafed and bombed planes dispersed around Nasuno and other fields north of Tokyo. Throughout the operation against Japan, *Lexington*'s pilots encountered no air opposition. The CAP encountered and splashed one "Jill" (Nakajima B6N Navy carrier attack bomber), CVG-94's only "kill."

After fueling on August 14, TG 38.1 returned to hit the Tokyo area the next day; one strike hit installations at Hyakurigahara, but a second strike received recall orders while en route to the target because the Japanese had surrendered. *Lexington* retired from the Tokyo area on August 16 and fueled. Two days later, she embarked Vice Adm. Frederick C. Sherman, Commander, First Carrier Task Force, Pacific, who used her as his flagship until August 20.

Lexington marked time until August 25, when she steamed to within a hundred miles of the coast of Honshu and began supporting the unfolding occupation of Japan. In the patrols carried out by *Lexington*'s planes over the northern neck of Honshu, her pilots located five prisoner of war (POW) camps. Consequently, *Lexington* planes dropped rations and other supplies to each camp. While similar patrols the next day revealed no additional POW facilities, *Lexington* dropped more supplies to three of the compounds she had come across the day before.

When TG 38.1 relieved TG 38.4 in the Tokyo area on August 29–30, *Lexington*'s planes patrolled the city, the waters of Tokyo Bay, the Kawasaki waterfront, and the Chiba Peninsula. She provided CAP for the movement of occupation forces into Tokyo and for General MacArthur as he landed at Atsugi airfield. *Lexington*'s planes also continued dropping supplies to POW camps. Reassigned then to TG 38.3, *Lexington* conducted patrols—including those over Tokyo Bay during the signing of the surrender accords on board the battleship *Missouri* on September 2—and POW supply missions until September 4. She entered Tokyo Bay the next day.

Lexington then carried out two days of patrols and POW supply missions over northern Honshu before returning to Tokyo Bay on September 10. After a brief period of rest and replenishment, she sailed to resume her work off Honshu on September 15. As transfers began to sap her of experienced and trained men, demobilized with the coming of peace, *Lexington* got under way for Saipan on September 21. Reaching her destination three days later, she received a new air group, CVG-92. *Lexington* sortied for Eniwetok later the same day and reached that atoll on September 27, where her crew enjoyed the first extensive leave and liberty since leaving the Philippines.

While spending much of the rest of 1945 in Japanese waters, *Lexington* remained fully active in a training role and did not take part in the "Magic Carpet" operations that returned servicemen stateside. After operating out of Pearl Harbor into mid-May 1946, she returned to the west coast, reaching San Diego on May 20. *Lexington* later steamed to San Francisco and Port Townsend, Washington. She was finally decommissioned and placed in reserve at Puget Sound on April 23, 1947.

Although *Lexington* remained inactive during the Korean War, a conflict in which several of her sister ships participated, she did return to active service as a result of that conflict. Reclassified as an attack aircraft carrier, CVA-16, on October 1, 1952, she was taken out of mothballs on September 1, 1953, to undergo extensive modernization at the Puget Sound Navy Yard. At that time, she received an enclosed bow similar to that in the new *Forrestal*-class carriers, a streamlined bridge,

Fig. 13. *Lexington*, her appearance dramatically altered by modernization during the 1950s, launches a Douglas AD-6 Skyraider of Attack Squadron (VA) 215 during the ship's Western Pacific (WestPac) deployment in 1961. Among the ship's more visible changes are the angled flight deck, enclosed "hurricane" bow, and completely restructured island. Other aircraft on her deck include the McDonnell F3H-2 Demon, North American FJ-4B Fury, and Douglas A3D-2 Skywarrior. *Courtesy U.S. Navy*

and an angled flight deck. Her No. 1 aircraft elevator was enlarged, and the No. 3 elevator was moved from the centerline to the starboard deck edge aft of the island, a relocation that left a clear landing area in the revised angled flight deck.

Recommissioned on August 15, 1955, *Lexington* departed Puget Sound on November 4 and reached her new home port of San Diego four days later. She resumed flight operations on January 9, 1956, when she launched and recovered a Grumman S2F Tracker. Following post-shakedown repairs and alterations at Puget Sound, *Lexington* returned to San Diego, whence she sortied on May 28, 1956, with Air Task Group 1 embarked. *Lexington* reached Pearl on June 2 on her first voyage to the Western Pacific (WestPac) since recommissioning, and she reached Yokosuka on June 25, 1956. Over the next three months, *Lexington* trained out of Yokosuka, Kobe, Buckner Bay, Iwakuni, and Sasebo, punctuated with a recreational visit

Fig. 14. A North American FJ-4B Fury of Attack Squadron (VA) 212 launches from *Lexington*'s port catapult on April 11, 1961, during the ship's deployment to the Western Pacific. *Courtesy National Archives*

to Hong Kong. *Lexington* returned to San Diego on October 18, via Pearl Harbor, and then shifted to Bremerton, arriving on November 7, to commence post-deployment repairs and alterations.

That deployment set the pattern for the next five years, as *Lexington* performed an important role in U.S. foreign policy, often in times of international tension. Between WestPac deployments, she qualified carrier pilots off the coast of southern California.

During her 1958 WestPac tour she operated with the Seventh Fleet to safeguard the Nationalist Chinese islands of Quemoy and Matsu, a vital role she repeated the following year. Between those operations, she remained on alert in the South China Sea as the United States deployed naval forces to protect national interests during the Laotian crisis in August

Fig. 15. Frontline fleet air squadrons often used *Lexington* to upgrade their skills during the ship's twenty-nine-year career (1962–91) as the navy's training carrier. Here a Grummen S-2D Tracker from Antisubmarine Squadron 30 takes off from the port catapult in January of 1963, while a second Tracker awaits launch in the right foreground. Bundled-up flight-deck crew members confirm the chilly time of year. *Courtesy U.S. Navy*

and September of 1959. Unrest in Laos in 1960 again saw *Lexington* operating with the Seventh Fleet into January of 1961.

As newer, more sophisticated carriers joined the fleet, however, *Lexington*'s time—and that of the other aging *Essex*-class ships—as a first-line carrier neared its end. After she proceeded via South America to the New York naval shipyard for an overhaul, arriving on September 24, 1962, *Lexington* was reclassified as an antisubmarine warfare carrier, CVS-16, on October 1.

Lexington was slated to relieve *Antietam* as the training carrier at Naval Air Station Pensacola on November 14, but international tensions over the discovery of Soviet missiles in Cuba dictated otherwise. As the United States and the Soviet Union stood on the brink of war, *Lexington* remained ready to perform in the attack carrier role, operating out of Mayport while engaged in refresher training and carrier qualification work. In the wake of the Cuban Missile Crisis, *Lexington* was

Fig. 16. Lt. Kathy P. Owens, left, made the last of a record 493,248 arrested landings on *Lexington* during the ship's forty-eight-year service career. Lieutenant Owens's husband, Lt. John Owens, right, joined his wife at the ship's formal decommissioning ceremony on November 8, 1991. *Courtesy U.S. Navy*

Fig. 17. *Lexington* is shown in profile from her port side in the late 1980s, near the end of her distinguished active service career. But the ship continues to serve, interpreting the history of naval aviation for thousands of visitors as the USS *Lexington* Museum on the Bay in Corpus Christi, Texas. *Courtesy U.S. Navy*

administratively assigned to the chief of naval air training on December 20, 1962, and relieved *Antietam* eight days later.

Reclassified CVT-16 on January 1, 1969, and to AVT-16 on July 1, 1978, *Lexington* operated out of Pensacola (Florida) for twenty-nine years. The ship averaged more than twenty thousand launches a year; carried out basic, advanced, and fleet pilot qualifications; and served as a visible representative of the navy's "people to people" programs. *Lexington* "showed the flag" at such places as New Orleans, Louisiana, and Port Aransas and Galveston, Texas. Her performance in the vital training role earned her a Meritorious Unit Commendation for the period from January 1, 1984, to August 21, 1986. She logged her 493,248th—and final—landing on March 8, 1991. On November 8, 1991, *Lexington* was decommissioned, more than half a century after Congress, prompted by a deteriorating world situation to build a navy second to none, appropriated the funds to construct her.

Viewing Plane of Inboard Profile

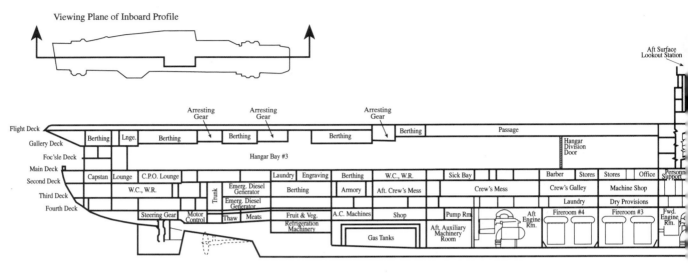

Flight Deck
Gallery Deck
Foc'sle Deck
Main Deck
Second Deck
Third Deck
Fourth Deck

Arresting Gear
Arresting Gear
Arresting Gear

Aft Surface Lookout Station

| Berthing | Lnge. | Berthing | Berthing | Berthing | Berthing | Passage | | Hangar Division Door | | | | | | Personnel Support |

Hangar Bay #3

| Capstan | Lounge | C.P.O. Lounge | | Laundry | Engraving | Berthing | W.C., W.R. | | Sick Bay | | | Barber | Stores | Stores | Office |

| W.C., W.R. | Trunk | Emerg. Diesel Generator | Berthing | Armory | Aft. Crew's Mess | Crew's Mess | Crew's Galley | Machine Shop |
| Emerg. Diesel Generator | | | | | | Laundry | Dry Provisions |

| Steering Gear | Motor Control | Thaw | Meats | Fruit & Veg. Refrigeration Machinery | A.C. Machines | Shop | Pump Rm | Aft. Auxiliary Machinery Room | Aft Engine Rm. | Fireroom #4 | Fireroom #3 | Fwd. Engine Rm. |
| | | Gas Tanks |

INBOARD PROFILE
(Present)

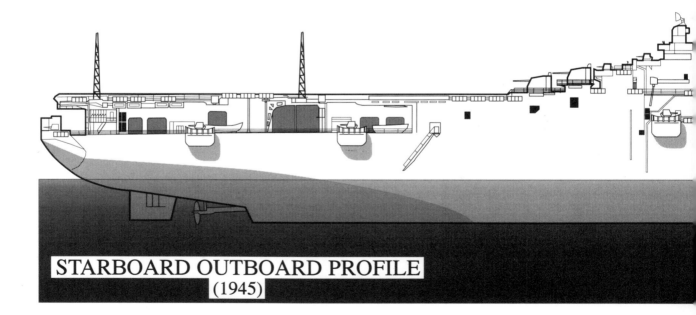

STARBOARD OUTBOARD PROFILE
(1945)

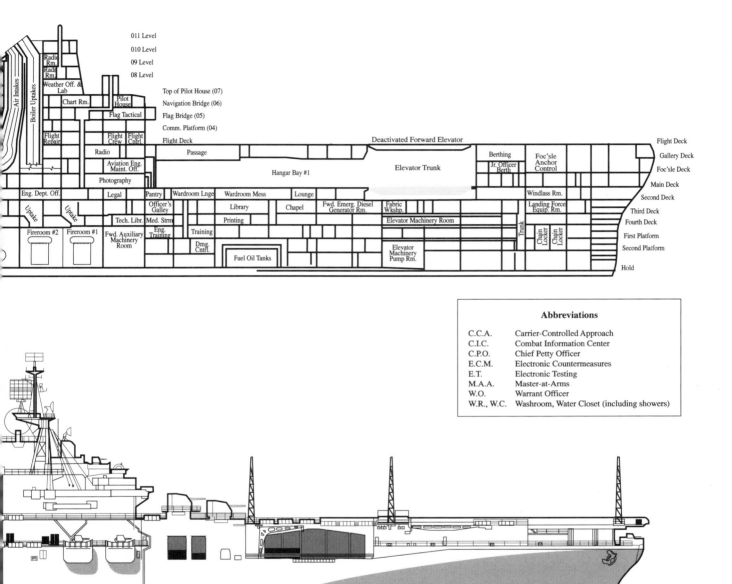

011 Level
010 Level
09 Level
08 Level

Top of Pilot House (07)
Navigation Bridge (06)
Flag Bridge (05)
Comm. Platform (04)

Radio Rm.
Radio Rm.
Weather Off. & Lab
Chart Rm.
Pilot House
Flag Tactical
Flight Repair
Flight Crew
Flight Cntrl.
Flight Deck
Radio
Passage
Aviation Eng. Maint. Off.
Photography
Eng. Dept. Off.
Legal
Pantry
Wardroom Lnge
Wardroom Mess
Lounge
Officer's Galley
Library
Chapel
Fwd. Emerg. Diesel Generator Rm.
Fabric Wkshp.
Tech. Libr.
Med. Strm
Printing
Elevator Machinery Room
Eng. Training
Fireroom #2
Fireroom #1
Fwd. Auxiliary Machinery Room
Training
Dmg. Cntrl.
Fuel Oil Tanks
Elevator Machinery Pump Rm.
Uptake
Uptake
Air Intakes
Boiler Uptakes

Deactivated Forward Elevator
Elevator Trunk
Hangar Bay #1
Berthing
Jr. Officer Berth
Foc'sle Anchor Control
Windlass Rm.
Landing Force Equip. Rm.
Trunk
Chain Locker
Chain Locker

Flight Deck
Gallery Deck
Foc'sle Deck
Main Deck
Second Deck
Third Deck
Fourth Deck
First Platform
Second Platform
Hold

Abbreviations	
C.C.A.	Carrier-Controlled Approach
C.I.C.	Combat Information Center
C.P.O.	Chief Petty Officer
E.C.M.	Electronic Countermeasures
E.T.	Electronic Testing
M.A.A.	Master-at-Arms
W.O.	Warrant Officer
W.R., W.C.	Washroom, Water Closet (including showers)

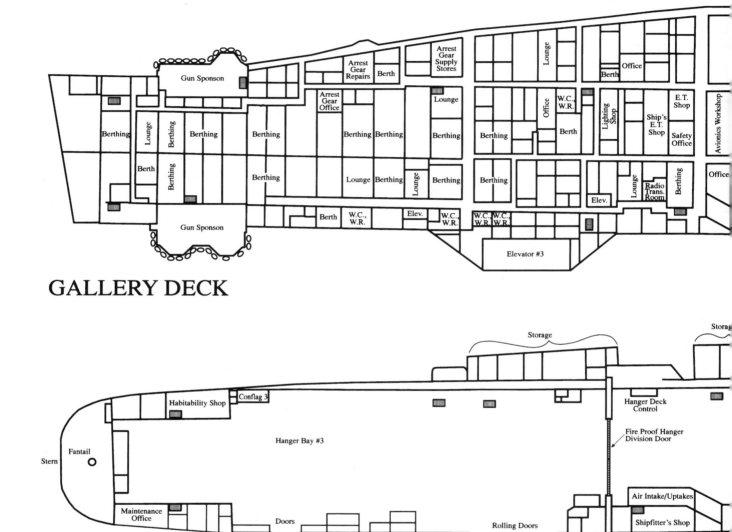

GALLERY DECK

Gun Sponson

Berthing | Lounge | Berthing | Berthing | Berthing | Berthing | Berthing

Berth | Berthing | Berthing | Lounge | Berthing | Lounge | Berthing | Berthing

Arrest Gear Repairs | Berth

Arrest Gear Office

Arrest Gear Supply Stores

Lounge

Lounge

Berthing

Berth | W.C., W.R. | Elev. | W.C., W.R. | W.C., W.R. | W.C., W.R.

Gun Sponson

Lounge

Office

W.C. W.R.

Berth

Lighting Shop

Ship's E.T. Shop

E.T. Shop

Safety Office

Avionics Workshop

Berth | Office

Lounge | Radio Trans. Room | Berthing | Office

Elev.

Elevator #3

HANGAR DECK

Storage

Storag

Habitability Shop

Conflag 3

Hanger Bay #3

Hanger Deck Control

Fire Proof Hanger Division Door

Stern

Fantail

Maintenance Office

Doors

Rolling Doors

Air Intake/Uptakes

Shipfitter's Shop

Deck Edge Elevator Hinged Platform

Fueling Station

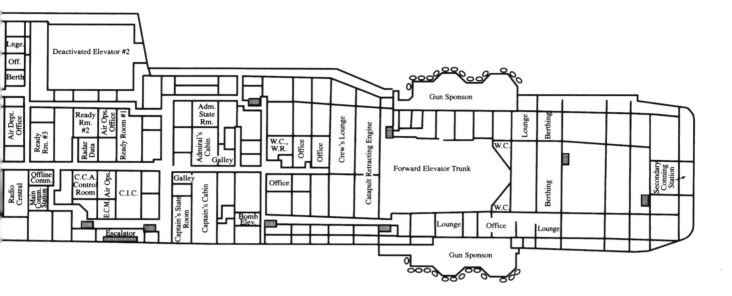

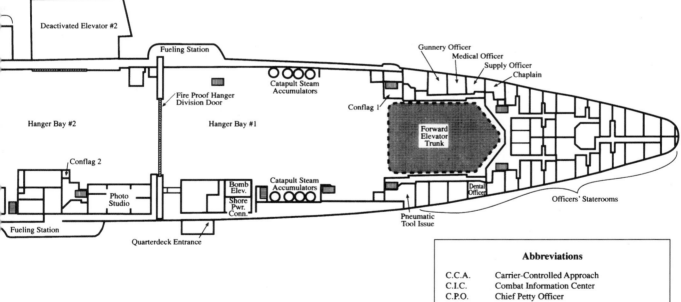

Abbreviations

C.C.A.	Carrier-Controlled Approach
C.I.C.	Combat Information Center
C.P.O.	Chief Petty Officer
E.C.M.	Electronic Countermeasures
E.T.	Electronic Testing
M.A.A.	Master-at-Arms
W.O.	Warrant Officer
W.R., W.C.	Washroom, Water Closet (including showers)

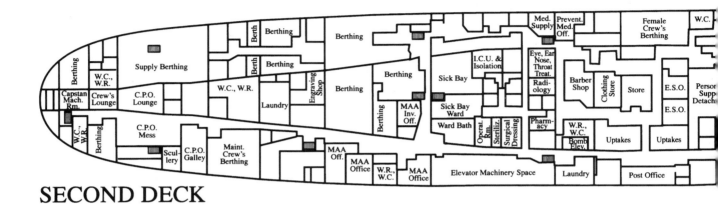

SECOND DECK

- Berthing
- W.C., W.R.
- Capstan Mach. Rm.
- Crew's Lounge
- Supply Berthing
- C.P.O. Lounge
- Berth
- Berthing
- Berthing
- Berth
- Berthing
- W.C., W.R.
- W.C., W.R.
- Berthing
- C.P.O. Mess
- Scullery
- C.P.O. Galley
- Maint. Crew's Berthing
- Laundry
- Engraving Shop
- Berthing
- Berthing
- MAA Off.
- MAA Office
- W.R., W.C.
- MAA Office
- Berthing
- Berthing
- Berthing
- MAA Inv. Off.
- Sick Bay
- Sick Bay Ward
- Ward Bath
- I.C.U. & Isolation
- Operat. Rm.
- Steriliz.
- Surgical Dressing
- Elevator Machinery Space
- Med. Supply
- Prevent. Med. Off.
- Eye, Ear, Nose, Throat Treat.
- Radiology
- Pharmacy
- Barber Shop
- Clothing Store
- Store
- W.R., W.C.
- Bomb Elev.
- Uptakes
- Laundry
- Female Crew's Berthing
- E.S.O.
- E.S.O.
- Uptakes
- Post Office
- W.C.
- Person. Supp. Detachm.

THIRD DECK

- Female C.P.O. Berthing
- Berthing
- Berthing
- Berthing
- C.P.O. W.C., W.R.
- C.P.O. Berthing
- C.P.O. Berthing
- Berthing
- Berthing
- Berthing
- Berthing
- Weight Room
- Berthing
- Armory
- Scullery
- Berthing
- Office
- Aft Crew's Mess
- Berthing
- Berthing
- Crew's Mess
- Crew's Mess
- Berthing
- Dental Dept.
- Dental Dept.
- Crew's Mess
- Crew's Mess
- Bakery
- Bomb Elev.
- Uptakes
- Veg. & Meat Prep. Rm.
- Crew's Galley
- Machine Shop
- Uptakes
- Berthing
- Female Crew's Berthing
- Boiler Shop
- Fem. Cre. Bert.

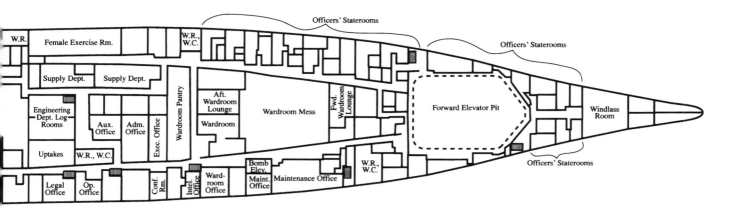

W.R.   Female Exercise Rm.   W.R., W.C.   Officers' Staterooms   Officers' Staterooms

Supply Dept.   Supply Dept.

Wardroom Pantry

Engineering Dept. Log Rooms   Aux. Office   Adm. Office   Exec. Office   Aft. Wardroom Lounge   Wardroom Mess   Fwd. Wardroom Lounge   Forward Elevator Pit   Windlass Room

Uptakes   W.R., W.C.   Wardroom

Legal Office   Op. Office   Conf. Rm.   Intel. Office   Wardroom Office   Bomb Elev.   Maint. Office   Maintenance Office   W.R., W.C.   Officers' Staterooms

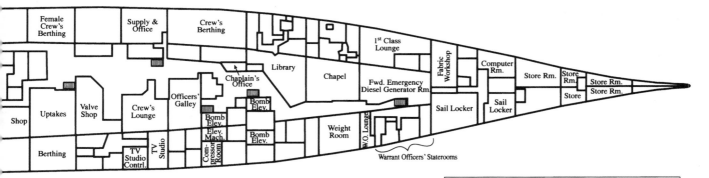

Female Crew's Berthing   Supply & Office   Crew's Berthing   1st Class Lounge   Fabric Workshop   Computer Rm.   Store Rm.   Store Rm.   Store Rm.

Library   Chapel   Store Rm.

Shop   Uptakes   Valve Shop   Crew's Lounge   Officers' Galley   Chaplain's Office   Bomb Elev.   Fwd. Emergency Diesel Generator Rm.   Sail Locker   Sail Locker   Store

Berthing   TV Studio Contrl.   TV Studio   Com-pressor Room   Elev. Mach.   Bomb Elev.   Bomb Elev.   Weight Room   W.O. Lounge   Warrant Officers' Staterooms

Abbreviations	
C.C.A.	Carrier-Controlled Approach
C.I.C.	Combat Information Center
C.P.O.	Chief Petty Officer
E.C.M.	Electronic Countermeasures
E.T.	Electronic Testing
M.A.A.	Master-at-Arms
W.O.	Warrant Officer
W.R., W.C.	Washroom, Water Closet (including showers)

PLATES OF *LEXINGTON*

The aircraft carrier USS *Lexington* (CV-16), seen from the break-water at her new home in Corpus Christi, Texas, is more than a memorial ship. The longest-serving aircraft carrier in U.S. naval history, the ship is also the longest-active member of the most numerous class of carriers built by the United States. As such, *Lexington* epitomizes the success of U.S. carrier design, which has left the United States the only country in the world operating large fleet carriers.

Lexington served for forty-eight years (1943–1991) and was the last to be decommissioned of twenty-four *Essex*-class carriers built during World War II. She was the second ship in the class to commission, at the South Boston Navy Yard on February 17, 1943. The ship was completed nearly two years ahead of schedule by its builder, Bethlehem Steel Shipyard, on the Fore River in Quincy, Massachusetts.

During construction, *Lexington* established a trend that would continue with other ships of the class. An earlier carrier *Lexington*, hull number CV-2 and also built at the Bethlehem yard, was sunk at the Battle of the Coral Sea on May 8, 1942. When the news reached Quincy, workers on hull CV-16, bearing the name *Cabot*, petitioned Sec. of the Navy Frank Knox to rename the ship for her lost predecessor; on June 16, 1942, CV-16 became *Lexington*. Thereafter, the name of each U.S. carrier lost in the war was transferred to an *Essex*-class hull under construction, with the exception of *Langley* (CV-1), which was given to a light fleet carrier (CVL-27).

Lexington was one of the most successful of all U.S. aircraft carriers. Serving exclusively in the Pacific, the ship's air groups destroyed more than a thousand Japanese aircraft in the air or on the ground, and they damaged or sank more than a million tons of Japanese naval and merchant shipping. *Lexington* earned eleven battle stars; only the fabled *Enterprise* (CV-6), of the preceding *Yorktown* class, and *Essex* (CV-9) earned more. Among twelve other operational awards, *Lexington* was one of only six U.S. carriers presented the coveted Presidential Unit Citation.

Lexington did not serve unscathed. Twice the ship was hit by Japanese planes, and 59 men were killed and 167 wounded. But the Japanese reported *Lexington* sunk four times. Because those reports mentioned a "great blue ship"—throughout the war, *Lexington* wore only a basic sea-blue paint scheme—the ship was known as the Blue Ghost throughout her career.

Among other wartime distinctions, *Lexington* served as the flagship of Task Force 58, under Vice Adm. Marc A. Mitscher, from March 8 to November 1, 1944. *Lexington*'s pilots had the satisfaction of sinking the Japanese carrier *Zuikaku*, whose planes had sunk the first *Lexington*. And CV-16 was the first American fleet carrier to enter Tokyo Bay, on September 5, 1945, after Japan formally surrendered on September 2.

This aerial view by Jim Cruz displays *Lexington*'s angled flight deck, one of the principal design improvements that enabled *Essex*-class carriers to serve the U.S. Navy through five more decades after World War II.

Originally a concept of the British Royal Navy, the angled deck allowed pilots a third option beyond "land or crash"; aircraft that missed the arresting wires had enough power to become airborne again and make a new attempt. The efficiency with which carriers operated their air groups improved dramatically after the introduction of the angled flight deck.

This was especially important as jet aircraft replaced propeller-driven planes after World War II. The slow-accelerating jet needed too much runway to make rolling takeoffs from carrier decks, and its landing speeds were too high for existing deck configurations and arresting gear. The U.S. carrier force, which ended World War II as the largest in the world, faced obsolescence unless improvements were made. As further impetus, the Korean War broke out in 1950; in the early weeks of the conflict, carrier-based air strikes were the only direct intervention available to the United States.

So the *Essex*-class carriers were modernized during the 1950s. *Lexington*, deactivated and in reserve since 1947, was designated an attack carrier (CVA-16) on October 1, 1952. On September 1, 1953, the ship entered the Puget Sound Navy Yard for modernization under the SCB-27C program.

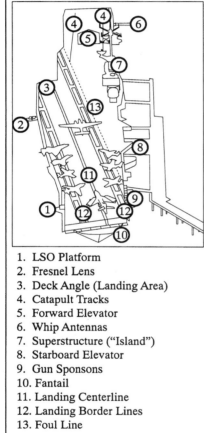

1. LSO Platform
2. Fresnel Lens
3. Deck Angle (Landing Area)
4. Catapult Tracks
5. Forward Elevator
6. Whip Antennas
7. Superstructure ("Island")
8. Starboard Elevator
9. Gun Sponsons
10. Fantail
11. Landing Centerline
12. Landing Border Lines
13. Foul Line

Other ships of the class had been modernized earlier under the SCB-27A program. But the angled deck and the development of steam catapults, which could launch aircraft twice as heavy as their World War II predecessors, made possible more radical changes on later modernizations. *Lexington* was one of the first three *Essex*es to undergo this complete transformation.

The ship's appearance changed dramatically. The superstructure, or "island," was streamlined; a heavy pole mast replaced the tripods; the gun system was completely replaced; side armor was removed and blisters added to increase the ship's beam; new radars were installed; and larger generators provided more electrical power.

The biggest changes involved aircraft operations. In addition to the angled deck and catapults, stronger arresting gear was installed. The forward centerline deck elevator was enlarged, the after one removed, and deck-edge elevators added port and starboard. The flight deck was strengthened, an enclosed "hurricane" bow was constructed, aviation fuel storage capacity was increased, and in keeping with the times, provision was made for storage and assembly of nuclear weapons.

PLATE 3: STERN VIEW

From astern, *Lexington* shows the pronounced overhang of the flight-deck landing angle. But the angled flight deck that was installed during modernization in 1953–55 changed more than the ship's profile. It extended *Lexington*'s service life to include continued major roles, such as deployment to the Pacific during the Cold War crises of the 1950s, deployment near Cuba during the missile crisis of 1962, and finally, designation as the navy's training carrier from 1962 to 1991, based at Pensacola, Florida. During *Lexington*'s training career, the ship established records unlikely ever to be broken, including 493,248 arrested landings, more than 227,000 launches from the starboard catapult, and carrier qualification of some 1,500 naval aviators each year. *Lexington*'s twenty-nine years as the navy's training carrier exceeds the combined training assignment periods of all her predecessors. *Lexington* is also the only U.S. carrier to have held five separate classifications during her service life: CV-16, a fast fleet carrier, in World War II; CVA, an attack carrier, 1955–62; CVS, antisubmarine carrier, 1962–69; CVT, training carrier, 1969–78; and finally, since 1978, the only U.S. carrier to hold the designation AVT.

PLATE 4: STERN PROFILE

This starboard-side view of the stern was the first closeup of *Lexington* that nearly half a million visitors saw during the ship's first year as the USS *Lexington* Museum on the Bay in Corpus Christi. The open area under the rear lip of the flight deck is the fantail, occupied during World War II by antiaircraft gun mounts. The sponsons on the side just below flight-deck level also held antiaircraft guns during the war. The racks hanging from the sponsons held lifeboat pods during *Lexington*'s career as a training carrier. The plane on the flight deck is an A3D Skywarrior. *Lexington* received her first battle damage in World War II in this starboard stern quarter, from a torpedo launched by a Japanese "Betty" twin-engined bomber just before midnight on Dec. 4, 1943. After the hit, the ship listed to starboard, lost steering control, and careened in a circle for more than twenty minutes as other ships in the formation maneuvered to avoid collision. A hand-operated hydraulic steering unit in the steering engine room was finally brought into operation, and the ship came under helm control thirty minutes after the torpedo hit. Casualties included nine dead and thirty-five wounded. *Lexington* returned to Pearl Harbor for temporary repairs under her own power, but steering with her engines. From Pearl, the ship proceeded to Bremerton, Washington, for permanent repairs, and was out of action until early February of 1944.

PLATE 5: MIDSHIPS VIEW

As visitors reach the summit of the long ramp leading to *Lexington*, the starboard elevator and the ship's superstructure (the island) come into view. Carrier elevators are used to transfer aircraft from the servicing areas of the hangar deck to the flight deck for launch. *Lexington*'s starboard unit, called a deck-edge elevator, continues in that role today and also serves as the main entrance for visitors. The island contains a carrier's primary command-and-control areas, and *Lexington*'s island was the scene of the ship's worst battle damage and casualties during World War II. By late 1944, Japan needed miracles in the Pacific, and they sought them from kamikaze ("divine wind" in Japanese) attacks, which were suicide dives into their targets by Japanese pilots. On November 5, 1944, while supporting ground operations on Luzon in the Philippines, *Lexington* was hit by a kamikaze that crashed into the 20mm antiaircraft gallery on the starboard rear side of the island. A tower of smoke rose from the site, and casualties were heavy: 50 dead and 132 injured. But the fires were brought under control within twenty minutes, flight operations continued uninterrupted, and *Lexington*'s gunners brought down another kamikaze headed for the carrier *Ticonderoga* (CV-14).

PLATE 6: FORESHIP VIEW

Seen from the quarterdeck end of *Lexington*'s entry ramp, the gray slab sides and enclosed bow of the ship tower above the waters of Corpus Christi Bay. Because of the need to operate aircraft in any weather, carriers from their inception had far greater freeboard—the height of the main deck above the water—than other types of warships. *Lexington*'s flight deck sits fifty-two feet above the ship's waterline, marked by the dark stripe at water level in this photograph. The area between the two rows of catwalks—called "walkarounds"— is the hangar deck, with seventeen and a half feet of clearance. The large doors in the side of the hangar deck are fire curtains that could be opened and closed automatically for damage control. *Lexington*, like all *Essex*-class carriers, began service with an open bow area, but bow and flight-deck damage to the carriers *Hornet* (CV-12) and *Bennington* (CV-20) during Pacific typhoons led to the installation of enclosed hurricane bows during the class modernization programs in the 1950s. *Lexington*'s bow was enclosed in 1953–55, with the flare of the hull blended into the forward end of the flight deck. The area occupied by the upper walkaround in this view contained massed batteries of antiaircraft weapons during World War II. During air operations, the counterweighted radio masts were rotated to a horizontal position to avoid obstructing the flight deck.

PLATE 7: SUPERSTRUCTURE (ISLAND) PROFILE

A noticeable change in *Lexington*'s profile after modernization involved the superstructure, or "island" in navy nomenclature. Early carriers, including the U.S. Navy's first, the *Langley* (CV-1), were "flush-deck" ships, with no superstructure. Naval aviators favored this design, since it offered minimum interference with flight operations. Command-and-control stations often were located forward along the sides of the flight deck, as in the early Royal Navy carrier HMS *Furious*. Exhaust gases from the boilers were vented through a variety of systems. *Langley* had a hinged stack that was lowered during flight operations; the Japanese *Akagi*, flagship of the Pearl Harbor attack force, had exhausts that curved down from the starboard side to vent away from the flight deck.

But flush-deck carriers were less desirable for ship commanders and non-aviation personnel, whose view eventually prevailed. By the late 1920s, carrier designs routinely included superstructures, and flight decks adjacent to them were widened to facilitate flight operations. Islands were usually located on the starboard side, because pilots preferred to make landing approaches from the port quarter.

On all *Essex*-class carriers, islands were completely replaced and streamlined during the SCB modernizations. Gone were the numerous antiaircraft guns and directors. The tripod mast was replaced by a single, heavy pole mast. The funnel was heightened and raked aft to vent away from the flight deck.

A portside profile of *Lexington*'s island shows several interesting features. Lower levels, including both bridges, were painted black to protect personnel from jet afterburner blast during launches. (This area has since been repainted gray.) The captain and staff ran the ship from the navigation bridge on the 06 level, while admirals and their staffs controlled fleet operations from the flag bridge one level lower, on 05. The catwalk aft of the navigation bridge is known as "Vulture's Row," because personnel watching operations from there had a clear view of flight-deck accidents and could be interviewed as part of any subsequent investigations.

The large "E" just below the funnel rim is for engineering excellence, earned by passing the biennial Operational Propulsion Plant Examination (OPPE). *Lexington* earned an "E" in both 1986 and 1988. Just below the "E," on the 08 level, is Pri-Fly, the priority flight control station, where the ship's "Air Boss" oversaw flight operations. The enclosed station below Pri-Fly held TV cameras that recorded flight deck operations. Located on the 07 level was the "weather shop," where the ship's meteorologists made and recorded observations, kept in touch with other weather sources, and created forecasts.

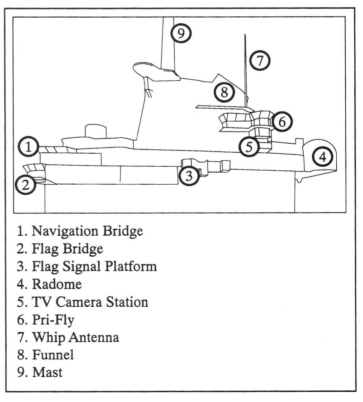

1. Navigation Bridge
2. Flag Bridge
3. Flag Signal Platform
4. Radome
5. TV Camera Station
6. Pri-Fly
7. Whip Antenna
8. Funnel
9. Mast

Even in noncombatant status, *Lexington* retained an impressive array of radar equipment, with the antennas located on the superstructure. Most are visible in this view. The two small antennas on top of the pilothouse are for Pathfinder navigation radar, a commercial unit with a range of ten miles, for maneuvering close to shore or in port. A receiver for these sets is located on the navigation bridge. One Pathfinder antenna sits atop the base of what was a Mark 25 gun director for the ship's post-1955 antiaircraft battery.

The antenna extending from the front of the mast belongs to the SPS–10 surface search radar, with a range of 15–100 miles. Directly opposite the SPS-10 is the antenna for the SPN-43 carrier controlled approach (CCA) radar, with a range of 120 miles. Flight controllers in the carrier air traffic control center (CATCC) used the SPN-43 to guide incoming aircraft to the carrier when visibility was poor.

Final approaches were handled by the SPN-35 radar, with its antenna in the bulbous radome (removed in 1995) at the aft end of the island. With a range of thirty-five miles, this unit provided precise information until pilots made visual contact with the carrier. Just forward of the radome was the SPN-12 airspeed indicator radar, which used Doppler shift measurement to determine final approach speeds.

The largest of *Lexington*'s radar antennas belongs to the SPS-40 two-dimensional air search radar, which could detect approaching aircraft up to two hundred miles away and could also determine their altitude—the "second dimension." *Lexington* was the first of the *Essex* class equipped with a height-finder, the prototype SM(CXBL), installed in March of 1943. The carrier battles of 1942, in which the United States lost five carriers, had shown the importance of altitude information in directing the ships' fighters.

Other wartime radars included SK air search; SG surface search; backup air search unit SC-2 and its improved successor, SR, the first of which was mounted in *Lexington*; and fire-control radar for the 5-inch and 40mm mounts. The *Essex* class also carried early electronic countermeasures (ECM) equipment to detect Japanese radar emissions, determine their direction, and jam the signals. Antenna arrangement was unique to each ship in the class, and it is often the key to identifying specific carriers.

1. Pathfinder Navigation Radars
2. SPS-10 Surface Search Radar
3. SPN-43 CCA Radar
4. SPN-35 Final Approach Radar
5. SPN-12 Doppler Air Speed Radar
6. SPS-40 Air Search Radar

PLATE 9: RIBBON BOARD

The ribbon board on the starboard side of *Lexington*'s navigation bridge displays the major operational awards won during the ship's career. *Lexington* is one of the most decorated ships in U.S. Navy history, with twelve operational citations and eleven World War II battle stars. Only *Enterprise* (CV-6), with twenty battle stars, and *Essex* (CV-9), with thirteen, earned more. *Lexington* was one of only six fleet carriers to earn the Naval Presidential Unit Citation, with one silver star, top left on the ribbon board. Other top row awards are the Navy Meritorious Unit Commendation, with two bronze stars; and the China Service Medal. On the second row, left to right, are the American Campaign Medal, with two silver stars and one bronze; the Asiatic-Pacific Campaign Medal; and the World War II Victory Medal. On the third row, left to right, are the Navy Occupation Service Medal; National Defense Service Medal, with two bronze stars; and Armed Forces Expeditionary Medal, with three bronze stars. The fourth row, left to right, includes the Coast Guard Special Operations Service Medal; Philippine Republic Presidential Unit Citation Badge; and the Philippine Liberation Ribbon. *Lexington*'s battle stars were earned for Pacific Raids–1943; Gilbert Islands Operations; Marshall Islands Operations; Hollandia Operation; Asiatic-Pacific Raids–1944; Marianas Islands Operations; Western Caroline Islands Operations; Leyte Operation; Luzon Operation; Iwo Jima Operation; and Third Fleet Operations against Japan.

PLATE 10: FLAG BOARD AND FOAM CANNON

Located on the port side of the island, along Vulture's Row, is one of *Lexington*'s two flag boards and a high-pressure foam cannon used in fighting fires on the flight deck. The flag board represents the oldest form of sending signals from one vessel to another at sea, and it remains in use today despite major advances in electronic communications. Flags are held in the board by oval metal rings attached to the top corner of the flag and gripped by spring releases in the board's "keys." Just above the flag board are the halyard lines, ascending to the crosstrees on the pole mast. Flag messages were run up on these lines by signalmen trained for speed and accuracy in composing such signals. When signals were ordered, the oval ring at the top corner of the first flag in the signal was connected to a clip on the halyard line. An identical clip attached to the bottom corner of the first flag was then hooked to the oval ring on the top corner of the next flag in the signal, and so on until the message was completed. There are individual flags for each letter of the alphabet, for digits, and for particular commands. Other flags contain entire messages, and groups of flags can be used to send messages by prearranged code. The foam cannon smothered fires with a chemically inert gas that separates oxygen from flammable fuels to prevent their ignition.

PLATES 11 AND 12: NAVIGATION BRIDGE AND PILOTHOUSE

The navigation bridge in these views is located on the 06 level of the superstructure and was the hub of command-and-control activity for the ship. *Lexington*'s navigation bridge was open during World War II, then was enclosed during the 1953–55 modernization. The windows are slanted forward to reduce glare, and each window section has its own wiper blade for foul weather conditions.

This area was the province of the ship's commanding officer, who holds the rank of captain in the United States Navy. His chair is shown at far left in the top photograph and at far right in the bottom one. From the bridge, the captain has direct communication with all departments and areas of the ship, as well as any admiral aboard on the flag bridge below. During air operations, the captain used a sound-powered black telephone located near his left hand to talk with the air officer, or Air Boss, in Pri-Fly. Both men had access to switches that control the flight-deck condition lights: green for a clear deck, red for foul. A large rear-view mirror, mounted just outside the bridge to the captain's left, gave him a clear view of the landing area, and he could view both launch and landing operations on a PLAT-TV monitor.

The near seat in the top view was occupied by the ship's navigator, and a third seat, out of sight and behind the captain's chair, was occupied by the operations officer. Located to the left of the navigator's chair is the monitor for the navigational radar, with a range of ten miles. Beyond the radar set are two identical clusters of instruments that indicate the ship's course and speed, wind direction and speed, and engine settings. One instrument cluster is located in front of the captain; the other is positioned in the center of the bridge for the officer of the deck (OOD)—a highly qualified junior officer who conns the ship under the direction of the commanding officer. Though guided primarily by the verbal and written commands of the captain, the OODs must be prepared to use their own judgment in emergencies.

The bottom photograph shows the front wall of the pilothouse, sometimes referred to in pre–World War II literature as the conning tower. The pilothouses on *Essex*-class carriers were armored, with 1.5 inches of special treatment steel (STS) on the roof and 1 inch on the sides. The porthole covers were closed during combat conditions to block the splinter fragments of near-miss explosions. The voice tube in the middle of the pilothouse wall connects to the flag plot on the 05 level below.

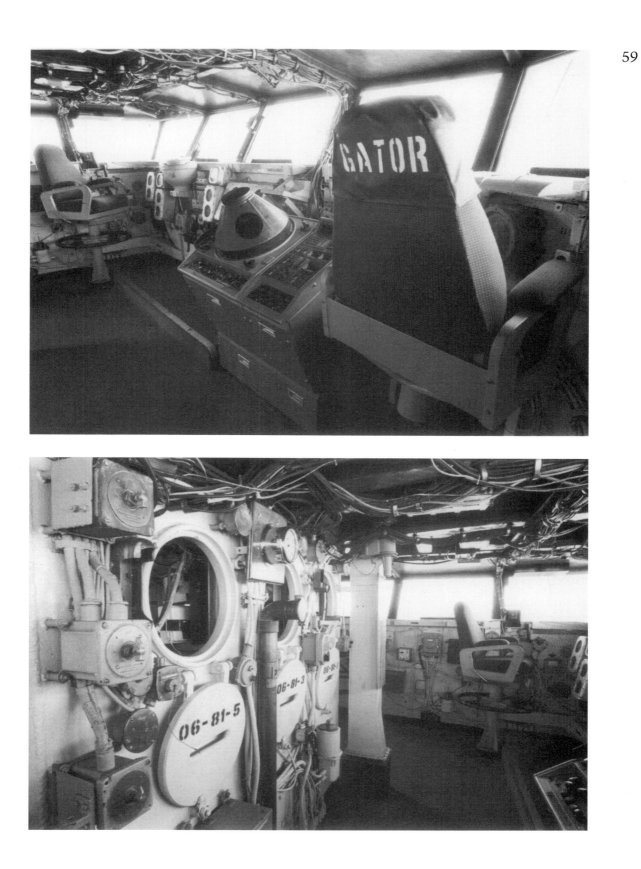

PLATES 13 AND 14: PILOTHOUSE INTERIOR AND SECONDARY CONN

At the center of the *Lexington*'s armored pilothouse are the primary instruments that control and monitor the movements and speed of the ship. At left is the engine order telegraph, which transmitted changes in the ship's speed to the engine room. Below the telegraph is the engine revolutions indicator, which displayed the ship's speed in revolutions per minute (rpms) of the propeller. These controls were manned by the lee helmsman, while the helmsman handled the helm wheel, at center, and tracked the ship's maneuvers on the rudder angle indicator and gyrocompass repeaters in front of him. At right is the brass compass binnacle, in which the ship's magnetic compass floats in alcohol.

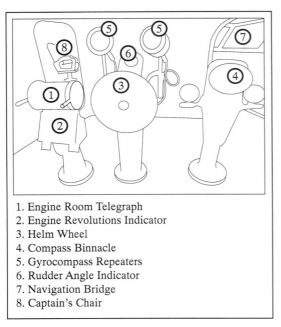

1. Engine Room Telegraph
2. Engine Revolutions Indicator
3. Helm Wheel
4. Compass Binnacle
5. Gyrocompass Repeaters
6. Rudder Angle Indicator
7. Navigation Bridge
8. Captain's Chair

Among other pilothouse personnel was the quartermaster, who was in charge of the ship's logbook, where he kept a complete written record of all orders and activity on the bridge. A bosun's mate piped or announced messages throughout the ship, over the 1-MC public address system, and several "talkers" with sound-powered phones relayed commands. Additional communications equipment included sirens; whistles; a pneumatic tube to the communications center; and collision, chemical, and general alarm switches.

All pilothouse personnel answered directly to the officer of the deck (OOD). When he gave a verbal order, it was repeated exactly by the appropriate pilothouse crew member, then repeated again when the order had been executed. Pilothouse personnel stood four-hour watches: 2400 hours to 0400 (4 A.M.) was the midwatch; 0400 to 0800 was the morning watch; 0800 to 1200 was the forenoon watch; 1200 to 1600 (4 P.M.) was the afternoon watch; 1600 to 1800 was the first dogwatch; 1800 to 2000 was the second dogwatch; and 2000 to 2400 (midnight) was the evening watch.

The bottom photograph shows the secondary conning station, located in the ship's bow just below the leading edge of the flight deck. A row of portholes in the compartment's forward wall offered personnel working here a view of every plane launched by *Lexington* during air operations. The equipment here was identical to that in the pilothouse; it included controls and monitors for the helm and engines, as well as communications links with the rest of the ship. During World War II, secondary conn was located in the island. It was moved forward after the bow was enclosed during the 1953–55 modernization. The ship's executive officer, second in command to the captain, was in charge of this station.

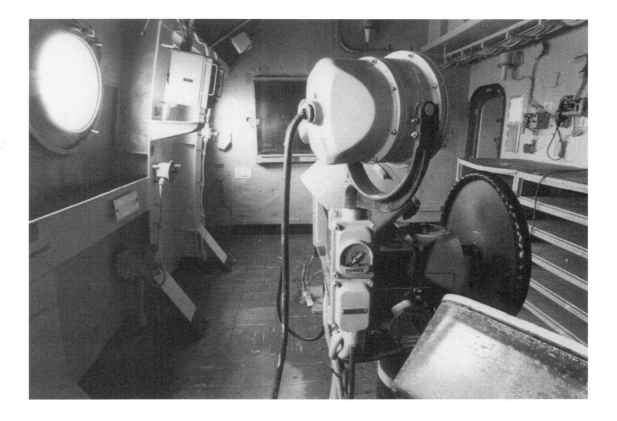

PLATE 15: CAPTAIN'S DAY CABIN

Although there is a luxurious (by warship standards) suite of rooms on the gallery deck, *Lexington* captains spent most of their time at sea in this small day cabin located on the navigation bridge, or 06, level in the ship's island. Despite its physical limitations, the day cabin had one overarching advantage: it kept *Lexington*'s ultimate decision-maker within a few steps of his station on the port side of the bridge.

By any standards, the day cabin is spartan. It contains a chair, a simple desk, a wall-mounted oscillating fan, a closet and small safe for valuables, a bed—note the raised "freeboard" that kept the captain from being tossed on the floor in rough weather—and a head with shower, at left. A telephone located adjacent to the bed on the back wall of the room provided instant access to the bridge. Another telephone was located on the inside wall of the head. Beyond the bulkhead opening lay the pilothouse and the navigation bridge. The captain could be there in seconds.

Thirty-three men commanded *Lexington*, beginning with Felix B. Stump, who served from the ship's commissioning in February of 1943 until April of 1944, when he was promoted to rear admiral commanding a division of escort carriers. In postwar years, Stump rose to admiral and commander-in-chief of the Pacific fleet (Cincpac) in 1953–58.

Ernest W. Litch commanded the ship from April of 1944 to January of 1945, a period when *Lexington* served as flagship of the fast carrier force in the two largest naval battles in history: the Battle of the Philippine Sea, also known as the Marianas Turkey Shoot, June 19–20, 1944; and the Battle of Leyte Gulf, October 23–26. Litch was promoted to vice admiral and also commanded a division of escort carriers after leaving *Lexington*.

Thomas H. Robbins, Jr., commanded the ship from the Okinawa campaign and the air strikes against the Japanese home islands through the end of the war. In the postwar navy, Robbins rose to the rank of rear admiral and was a key advisor to Sec. of the Navy James Forrestal, who oversaw the final transition to an "air navy." Robbins was replaced in November of 1945 by Bradford E. Crow, who served during the ship's deactivation period from May to October of 1946.

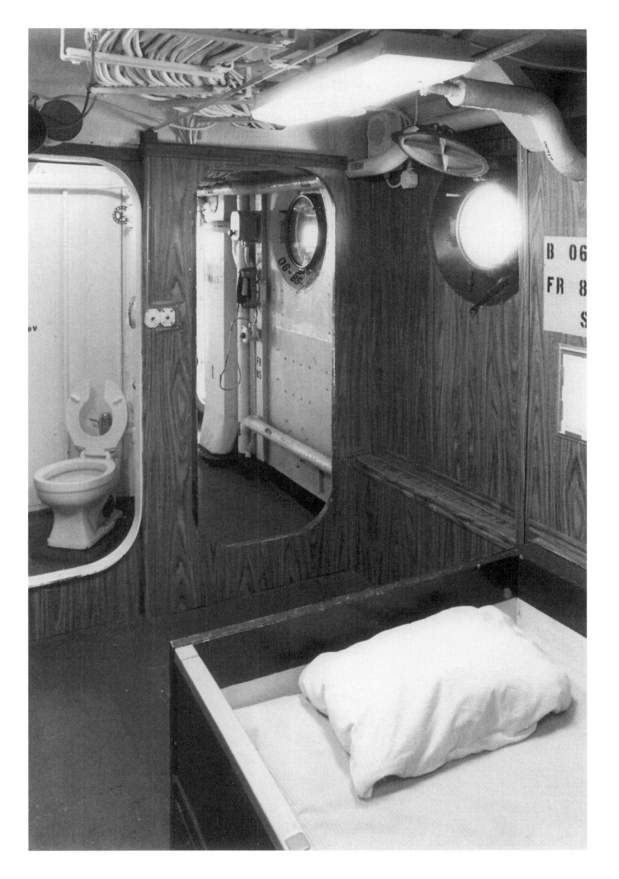

PLATE 16: CHART ROOM

Just aft of the captain's day cabin is the chart room, connected directly to the pilothouse and bridge by a corridor on the port side of the island. This area was the realm of the navigator, and despite the many modern electronic and automatic navigation systems, the navigator and quartermaster were kept busy using manual and celestial navigation systems as backups. Most of that work took place on chart tables like the one in the foreground. The cabinet-sized computer at the far left is a long-range navigation (LORAN) radar, and LORAN display units are located in the pilothouse and the combat information center (CIC). The rectangular brass plate just above the table on the far wall contains and protects the ends of primary cables. In commission, *Lexington*'s chart room equipment included a dead reckoning tracer (DRT), which automatically traced the ship's course and speed on charts or paper; inertial navigation sets; and more recently, a Global Positioning System (GPS) receiver, linked to U.S. observation satellites miles above the oceans. *Lexington*'s precision clocks, or chronometers, are also mounted in the chart house, where they were wound and checked daily. "Winding" the chronometers was part of the official noon report to the captain.

PLATE 17: FLAG BRIDGE

There are no clusters of instruments on the flag bridge, located on the 05 level, below the navigation bridge in *Lexington*'s island. This was "Admiral's Country," and the problems solved here were not about one ship, but scores of them. *Lexington* was often a flagship of task forces, for example, TF 58; and of smaller task groups, with designations like TG 58.1. The ship's most prominent flag status came from March to November of 1944, under Vice Adm. Marc A. Mitscher, commander of Task Force 58, which included all the fast fleet carriers in the Pacific at that time. It was aboard *Lexington* that Mitscher made the momentous and daring decision to turn on the lights of the task force—thereby exposing it to night attack—after darkness fell on June 20, 1944, to guide home the planes that had flown the final air strikes against the Japanese fleet in the Battle of the Philippine Sea. The flag bridge was open in World War II, and Mitscher, known as an "aviator's admiral," spent much of his time on the port wing of the bridge, where he could watch the launch and recovery of aircraft. Behind the flag bridge is the flag plot, which contained all the navigation equipment and charts for tactical planning, and the communications equipment for staying in touch with the rest of the task force ships.

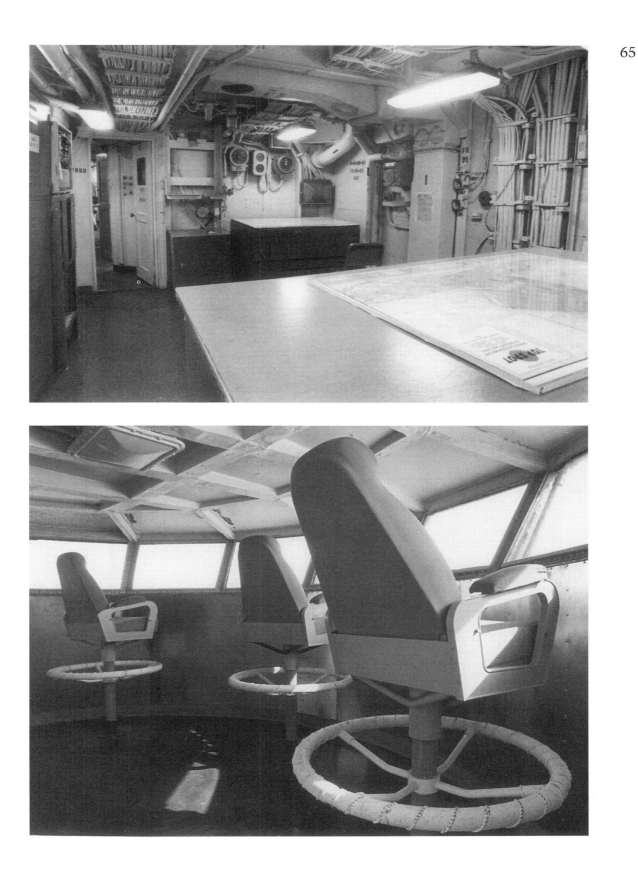

Located above and aft of the navigation bridge, on the 08 level of *Lexington*'s island, is primary flight control, or Pri-Fly, the equivalent of the control tower at a major airport. From Pri-Fly, the air officer, or "Air Boss," oversaw and directed the delicate and dangerous ballet carried out on *Lexington*'s flight deck. In the top view, the air officer occupied the left seat, and his top subordinate, the "Mini Boss," occupied the right. Both faced the ship's port side with a view that took in the entire flight deck.

Flight operations began with an announcement from the air officer to prepare the deck for launch, followed shortly by the order to start aircraft engines. From that point, the air officer had control of all air operations on the ship, including those of the flight deck, hangar deck, catapult and arresting gear compartments, as well as the air operations (AirOps) and carrier air traffic control center (CATCC) on the gallery deck. Pri-Fly personnel also monitored radar approaches, coordinated with the captain and the landing signals officer (LSO), and set hydraulic pressure for the arresting gear. Pri-Fly offered the best view—and the most demanding tasks—on a carrier.

The angled flight deck in the aerial view by Jim Cruz is all the space the air officer had to work with. *Lexington*'s flight deck is 910 feet long and 142 feet wide at the leading edge of the deck angle. The angled landing area is 520 feet long and oriented 13 degrees off the centerline of the ship's keel. The flight deck contains 90,000 square feet of space, which is enough to park a thousand automobiles but never quite enough to handle easily all the aircraft it needed to. The dark surface of the deck is a rubberized, abrasive, anti-slip coating with a thickness of one-quarter to one-half of an inch.

Lexington's World War II flight deck was a long rectangle with parallel sides, but progress changed that symmetry. Jets made necessary a landing area that was separate from the takeoff area. In theory, the angled deck made launches from the starboard catapult possible while aircraft were landing on the deck angle. The first true angled deck was fitted in 1952 on the *Antietam* (CV-36)—one of *Lexington*'s sister ships, and the ship *Lexington* replaced in 1962 as the navy's training carrier.

The single stripe of alternating yellow and white segments that ends at the forward edge of the deck angle is the landing centerline, and every landing procedure was designed to put the aircraft on that line. The twin white lines are the landing area boundaries, and the thin broken line is the foul line. All deck area to the port side of the foul line had to be clear of obstructions before the LSO got the green light to land aircraft.

PLATE 20: FLIGHT DECK DETAILS

The port edge of *Lexington*'s flight deck, forward of the landing angle, offers a view of some interesting details. The entire flight deck is ringed with safety nets, constructed of synthetic mesh, like those shown here. One of several new dangers that arrived on carrier flight decks with jet aircraft was the possibility of being blown overboard by the force of a plane's afterburners, which are at full throttle during launch operations. Just below the nets are the walkarounds that line both sides of the flight deck and provide quick access to the gallery deck immediately below.

The platform with the closed boxes just forward of the nets is the port deck-edge catapult launch station, and just beyond that are the port forward gun sponsons. The sponsons held 40mm Bofors anti-aircraft gun mounts in World War II, and either 5-inch/38-caliber single mounts or dual 3-inch/50s following the 1953–55 modernization. The aircraft on the flight deck is a PV-2D Harpoon, a twin-engine patrol bomber that performed valuable work for the navy during World War II, though it never operated from carriers (see aircraft plate A4). The safety fence was installed on *Lexington* after she became a museum ship in Corpus Christi.

The bend in the safety fence outlines one of the undulations of the flight deck, which has changed dramatically since World War II. *Lexington*'s original flight deck measured 862 by 108 feet and was constructed of teak or fir. The planks were bolted in place, and the counter-sunk bolt holes were filled for a smooth surface. Wooden flight decks were standard in American carrier designs and were intended to reduce top weight and improve stability, both of which were critical factors when dealing with battle damage. Portions of the wood can still be seen today, along the deck edges and away from major traffic and impact areas.

The modern angled deck measures 910 by 142 feet and has embedded landing lights, like those of an airport runway, and embedded PLAT-TV camera lenses that provide a view of both landings and launches. Also embedded in the flight deck are small, circular openings containing metal crossties. These are the tie-downs for parked aircraft, and they are also noticeable on the starboard deck-edge elevator and the hangar-deck floor. The flight deck contains expansion joints, one forward and two aft of the superstructure, that give the deck flexibility, which is crucial in avoiding damage in rough, open water.

PLATES 21A AND 21B: 40MM AND 20MM ANTIAIRCRAFT MOUNTS

Though unarmed today, *Lexington* bristled with the gun systems shown here during World War II. At top is a quad (four-barreled) 40mm antiaircraft mount, designed by Bofors of Sweden. The bottom photograph shows a single 20mm antiaircraft mount, designed by the Swiss firm of Oerlikon. Both were built by the United States under license.

Lexington also carried twelve 5-inch/38-caliber guns: eight of them in two pairs of superimposed twin turrets, one pair forward and one pair aft of the superstructure; and four guns as open single mounts in port-side sponsons. The 5-inch/38 was useful against level or torpedo bombers. For dive-bombers, automatic weapons were the answer. By the time the first *Essex*es commissioned, five of the navy's eight prewar carriers had been lost, and carrier captains were lobbying hard for increased antiaircraft protection.

In initial designs, *Lexington* and her sister ships mounted four quad 1.1-inch machine cannon, nicknamed "Chicago Pianos." These had a tendency to jam at high rates of fire, and by August of 1941 they were replaced by the 40mm Bofors, and the four mounts had increased to eleven. By May of 1945, *Lexington* showed fifteen 40mm mounts, and some *Essex*-class ships carried as many as eighteen. The mounts offered manual or power operation, and required a crew of ten. The guns fired a 1.9-pound shell at a muzzle velocity of 2,890 feet per second (fps) to a surface range of more than five miles and an antiaircraft ceiling of 22,800 feet at 90 degrees elevation. Maximum rate of fire was 160 rounds per minute.

Close air defense was first assigned to .50-caliber machine guns, with anywhere from ten to forty weapons planned. By August of 1941, this weapon was also inadequate against modern aircraft. Forty-six single 20mm mounts were substituted, in a tribute to the reputation that gun had earned aboard British warships in the Mediterranean. By May of 1945, *Lexington* mounted twenty-eight dual 20mm mounts, after the single mount failed to stop Japan's kamikazes. The 20mm mounts required a single gunner, assisted by several ammunition handlers. The shell weighed more than a quarter of a pound, with a muzzle velocity of 2,740 feet per second and a fire rate of 450 rounds per minute. Surface range exceeded 2 miles, and antiaircraft range was 10,000 feet at 90 degrees elevation. In a further attempt to stop the kamikazes, *Lexington* in 1945 carried six army Mark 31 .50-caliber quadruple machine gun mounts.

Fire control for this array was complex, since gun directors occupied space that sometimes conflicted with flight operations. *Lexington* began service with Mark 37 directors for the 5-inch mounts and Mark 49 and 51 directors for the automatic weapons. By May, 1945, the ship retained two Mark 37s and mounted nineteen radar-equipped Mark 57 directors. After recommissioning in 1955, *Lexington* carried a mix of single 5-inch/38s in open sponsons and 3-inch/50s in twin mounts, the latter designed in 1945 to replace the quad Bofors against the kamikazes.

PLATE 22: DECK-EDGE CATAPULT CONTROL STATION

Angled flight decks were the most visible adaptation of the carrier to the jet age, but equally important—though less visible—was the steam catapult. The view at right approximates the moment before launch from *Lexington*'s catapults, seen from the portside deck-edge catapult control station. Two A4 Skyhawks are positioned on the catapult tracks.

Like the angled deck, early steam catapult development was the work of the British Royal Navy, which first used it in 1949 on the carrier HMS *Perseus*. If the deck angle solved landing difficulties, the catapult solved the more fundamental problem of getting jets airborne from carrier flight decks. The catapult was not new. By the end of World War II, it was estimated that 40 percent of U.S. carrier launches were by catapult. *Lexington* and her sister ships were designed with two H4 hydraulic catapults on the flight deck and a double-action athwartships catapult that launched through both sides of the hangar deck. But *Lexington* commissioned with only the starboard H4. The port-side unit was added during repairs to the torpedo damage of December, 1943. The hangar-deck catapult was never installed.

But hydraulic catapults were not powerful enough to launch the new, heavier jets. Steam was the answer. *Lexington*'s H4s could launch an 18,000-pound aircraft at 90 knots down a 96-foot track. The improved H8s of the *Midway* class could manage 28,000 pounds at 90 knots. C11 steam catapults could launch 39,000 pounds at 136 knots, or 70,000 pounds at 107.5 knots, down a 211-foot track. And since steam power, measured in pounds of pressure per square inch (psi), could be varied according to the weight of the plane, less wind was needed across the flight deck to achieve lift. *Lexington* was one of the first six *Essex*es to receive C11s during its SCB-27C modernization in 1953–55.

During launch operations, flight-deck directors oversaw starting the engines, then guided the pilots in taxiing the aircraft over the catapult track. The wings were spread, flaps set and the jet blast deflector (JBD) raised behind the aircraft as the carrier turned into the wind and reached launch speed. The plane was attached to the catapult shuttle ramp by a "bridle," a holdback T-bar was attached to the rear of the fuselage, the bridle was tensioned and the engine was run up to full throttle. When the catapult officer got the green light, he swept his arm down to touch the deck, the signal for the deck-edge operator, standing with his hands above his head, to push the fire button on the center console. Below the flight deck, the "Fire" switch on the catapult control console was activated, and the launch valves on the thrust unit just below the flight deck opened. The holdback bar broke, and in three seconds, the aircraft was hurled clear of the flight deck.

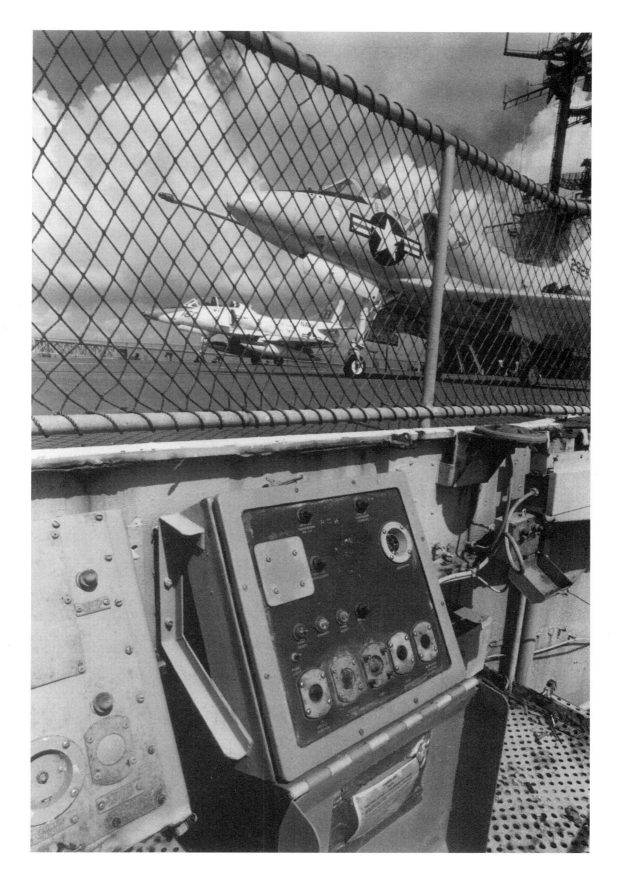

PLATES 23A AND 23B: CATAPULT RETRACTING ENGINE AND DIAGRAM

The steam catapult is a marvel of engineering ingenuity, though not simplicity, as these illustrations attest. The top view shows some of the hydraulic equipment that fills the catapult room on *Lexington*'s gallery deck. The bottom line drawing shows the main assembly elements of the catapult as it is mounted below the flight deck. Though steam was the driving force of *Lexington*'s catapults, hydraulics played a large role in positioning the catapult mechanism, retrieving it, and most important, activating the maze of valves that released steam to launch the aircraft.

The catapults consist of two slotted cylinders, eighteen inches in diameter, lying in a trough below the flight deck catapult track. Each cylinder contains a six-foot power piston, with a pointed retardation probe at the end toward the ship's bow. Both pistons are connected by keyed joints, resembling large zipper teeth, to a shuttle, which fits between the deck plates and rides on eight rollers down the catapult track guide rails on the flight deck. On the shuttle is a towing block, protruding between the guide rails. A ramp connects to the towing block. The shuttle, block, and ramp transmit the motion of the pistons to the aircraft by means of the bridle, attached to the ramp and to the plane's fuselage near the nose.

At the after end of the pistons is a large thrust unit, which held the built-up steam pressure (600 psi at 850°F). Steam was drawn directly from the ship's boilers, and the console operator "dragged" the steam into the thrust unit via the steam accumulators located on the port and starboard walls of hangar-deck bay 1. Hydraulic launching valves are located on the back of the thrust unit, and when the catapult was "fired" by the deck-edge operator, the launching valves were opened by a series of hydraulic valves known as a positive displacement system. When the launch valves opened, steam pressure in the thrust unit forced the pistons down the track, and the aircraft was carried along, its engines already at full throttle, until it cleared the end of the flight deck.

As the plane launched, the bridle was jerked free by the bridle arrester engine and cables, which lay alongside the catapult track and extended into the "bridle catchers," the horn-like booms protruding from the forward edge of the flight deck. The power pistons were halted at the forward end of the track by two water brake cylinders, which accepted the retardation probes of the pistons. The counterpressure of the water prevented metal-to-metal contact. The pistons and shuttle were retrieved for the next shot by a cable system and movable cart, called a GRAB. Exhausted steam was vented over the side of the ship through a hydraulic exhaust valve.

The catapult's hydraulic system was always charged, and 300 psi of steam pressure was maintained under a 24-hour steam watch, which was stood in four-hour shifts.

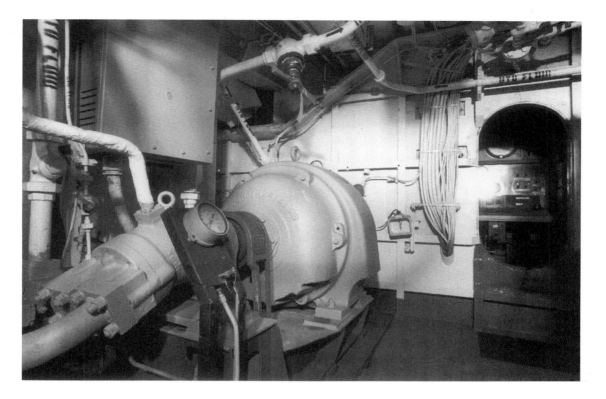

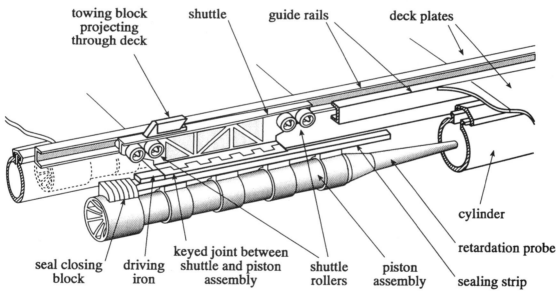

towing block
projecting
through deck

shuttle

guide rails

deck plates

cylinder

retardation probe

seal closing
block

driving
iron

keyed joint between
shuttle and piston
assembly

shuttle
rollers

piston
assembly

sealing strip

PLATES 24 AND 25: LSO PLATFORM AND OPTICAL LANDING SYSTEM (OLS)

The landing signals officer (LSO) platform aboard *Lexington*, top, can have a crowd on it and still be the loneliest place on board. This is because any LSO on the platform is the final link between the ship and the pilot of a high-performance aircraft who wants to land—in what has been called a controlled crash—on the ship's flight deck.

The LSO platform is located, as it was in World War II, on the port side, aft, a few yards from the rear edge of the flight deck. From here, the LSO controlled a modern version of the brightly colored paddles used to direct landings during the war. Today's "paddles" are the optical landing system (OLS), shown in the bottom view. The OLS is also located on the port side, some distance beyond the LSO platform but aft of the forward edge of the deck angle. It protrudes farther from the side of the ship to ensure that the pilot has a clear view of it at all times. All aircraft carrier landings are made visually, regardless of whether the approach is visual or directed by radar from the carrier air traffic control center (CATCC).

The LSO is a naval aviator, and a different LSO was on the platform for each type of aircraft in the traffic pattern. The LSO worked from the control panel, the covered box in the lower left corner of the top view, which contains a Doppler radar display of the plane's true approach speed, the PLAT-TV screen, a radar monitor, wind gauges, OLS controls, and a hook/ramp clearance indicator. A second panel contains two radios for communication with the aircraft, each using ten preset channels to simplify frequency changes made by either the LSO or the pilot. The windscreen protected the LSO's back, and speakers from the ship's MC (public address) system and a telephone for internal communications are also mounted on the screen. Alongside the platform is a safety net of synthetic mesh, into which the LSO could "bail out" if a landing got out of control. Each approach and landing were graded by the LSO and reported to the appropriate squadron.

The OLS was switched on when the captain, air officer, arresting gear officer, and LSO agreed that the deck was "green," that is, safe for a landing. Final approach began at "meatball acquisition," when the pilot saw clearly the orange "meatball" of the fresnal lens, which is the vertical center portion of the OLS. The lens gave the pilot vertical reference to the ship's deck, to ensure the plane was not too low on its approach. Green datum lights on either side of the meatball provided horizontal reference. The pilot's task was to fly an approach that kept the orange and green signals properly aligned. He or she was in constant radio contact with the LSO, who helped guide the descent and used a third set of lights on the OLS to signal "Land," "Cut" (cut engines), or "Wave off." Either the LSO or the air officer in Pri-Fly could signal a wave-off.

PLATES 26A AND 26B: TAILHOOK AND ARRESTING GEAR

The final step in the cycle of operating aircraft from a carrier has not changed much since the era of post–World War I ships with superstructures in the center of their flight decks. Aircraft must still snag a wire stretched across the deck. Through World War II, missing those wires meant a headlong plunge into a barrier to avoid crashing into parked aircraft, or going over the side, which was nearly always fatal.

Snagging the arresting wire is called a "trap" aboard U.S. carriers. It involves a tailhook, mounted at the rear of the plane, and the arresting system itself. The top view at right shows a tailhook in the down position under an A4 Skyhawk aboard *Lexington*. The close-up shows the poured zinc terminal through which the arresting wires are "run out" and retracted.

Early arresting systems often involved both longitudinal and transverse wires, plus a last-ditch barrier. In the 1920s, the British Royal Navy briefly dispensed with arresting gear altogether, preferring friction gear or a ramp-like rise in the aft flight deck to slow the aircraft. But the United States Navy parked aircraft on its flight decks, and that made arresting gear a required fixture on American carriers.

Lexington commissioned with the Mark IV arresting system and twelve wires, or "pendants"—six aft and six forward of the island. The latter group was part of the requirement that *Essex*-class carriers be able to land aircraft over the bow. Jets brought the Mark VII system, with six pendants, installed in 1955 and retained to decommissioning with a now-standard four pendants.

Pendants are 1 7/16 inches in diameter, with six thirty-wire strands around a hemp center. They are replaced after eighty traps, or if cut or frayed; a quick disconnect system allows changes in one minute. The pendants are suspended four inches above the flight deck by leafspring supports called "fiddle bridges." They are secured port and starboard through the terminals to the purchase cable, which is attached to the arresting engine on the gallery deck. The purchase cable is the same diameter as the pendant, with six twenty-five-wire strands around a hemp center, and is good for three thousand landings.

The arresting engine could theoretically absorb 29,300,000 foot-pounds of energy at peak fluid pressure and maximum cable runout of 250–300 feet. That could stop a 50,000-pound aircraft landing at 105 knots in 228 feet. Engine hydraulic resistance was set in Pri-Fly and varied with the type of aircraft.

Lexington's angled flight deck allowed an aircraft missing the wires to "touch and go" and make another attempt. Such a plane is called a "bolter." When the tailhook—lowered by the pilot—engaged a pendant, the aircraft slowed to a stop, then rolled back a few feet to disengage the pendant. If it did not, a hook runner entered the landing area to disengage it. The tailhook was then raised and the pendant was retracted, inspected, and positioned for the next recovery.

PLATES 27A AND 27B: STARBOARD ELEVATOR

The elevators are another of the more visible changes in aircraft carriers, both in *Lexington* and in overall carrier design. These two views show the starboard deck-edge elevator, at flight-deck level in the upper photograph and at hangar-deck level in the lower, where the elevator forms part of the visitors' entrance to the ship.

This elevator did not appear on *Lexington* until the 1953–55 modernization, when it replaced the aft centerline flight-deck elevator. At that time, *Lexington* retained her forward flight-deck elevator, but deck-edge elevators were installed on the port side at the front of the deck angle, and starboard, aft of the island. After reassignment as the navy's training carrier in 1962, *Lexington* had no permanently embarked air group and did not require three elevators. So the port deck-edge elevator was locked in place in the 1970s, becoming part of the landing area. The flight-deck elevator is also now locked in place.

Lexington's elevator layout during preliminary design called for three flight-deck elevators, fore and aft on the centerline with the midships elevator offset to starboard to avoid obstructing aircraft movement on the hangar deck. But the midships elevator continued to pose design problems, and in December of 1940, following the success of a prototype deck-edge unit aboard the small carrier *Wasp* (CV-7), designers moved the midships elevator to the port deck edge. The unit could be rotated to a vertical position, both to close the large opening it created in the side of the hangar deck and to facilitate passage through the Panama Canal. Today, all United States Navy carriers use only deck-edge elevators, with three on the starboard side and one to port aboard the 90,000-ton, nuclear-powered ships of the *Nimitz* class.

The operating cycle of the elevators during World War II was forty-five seconds, which was the interval required to lift a plane from the hangar to the flight deck, off-load it, and return to the hangar. But by the late 1940s, the 28,000-pound maximum lift capacity of *Lexington*'s elevators was totally inadequate for the much larger jet aircraft coming into service. The new deck-edge elevators added during her modernization provided a 57,000-pound lift capacity on the starboard elevator and a 46,000-pound capacity on the port unit. Both were 56 feet by 44 feet. The starboard elevator, like its World War II forerunner on the port side, can be rotated to a vertical position. All *Lexington*'s elevators used hydraulic power and were operated from the main hangar-deck control station in bay 2.

PLATE 28: HANGAR DECK

Though smaller than the flight deck, the cavernous appearance of *Lexington*'s hangar deck seldom fails to impress visitors. Unchanged in size since World War II, the hangar deck measures 654 feet by 70 feet, is 17.5 feet high, and covers 40,000 square feet. The plane is a Grumman TBF Avenger torpedo bomber (see aircraft plates A5 and A6).

The hangar deck is divided into three bays that could be sealed off by electrically operated fire doors. Each bay contains its own conflagration (CONFLAG) station for damage control, and bay 2 also contains the hangar-deck control station, located on the port wall, which oversaw all movement of aircraft and equipment on the hangar deck.

The floor of the hangar deck is covered by 1.5 inches of special treatment steel (STS) armor. It is the uppermost armored deck and the main strength deck of the *Lexington*, and it is numbered deck 1. Deck 4, above the vital machinery spaces, also provides 1.5 inches of STS to protect the ship's vitals. Early in the design of the *Essex* class, an armored flight deck had much appeal. British carriers were built with armored flight decks, but the cost was a reduction of 30–40 percent in the number of planes that the United States Navy considered optimum for carrier operations. A second but important consideration was the increase in top weight, which reduced the ship's stability, a key component of surviving battle damage.

For both reasons, the navy chose instead to armor the hangar deck sufficient to stop a 500-pound bomb. The armored fourth deck met the upper edge of the ship's armored belt, which tapered from 4 to 2.5 inches in thickness, was 10 feet deep, and covered 508 feet of the carrier's 820-foot waterline length. The side armor was designed to stop cruiser shell fire, and most of it was removed during the ship's 1953–55 modernization.

U.S. carrier operational philosophy has always included parking many of the ship's aircraft on the flight deck, so the hangar deck is seen more as a servicing than a storage area. On board *Lexington*, the heaviest maintenance work was handled in hangar bay 3, the largest and aftermost bay, with workshops and overhead hoists lining its walls. Since it was the only bay that could be "blacked out" completely, night maintenance was done here. After 1955, bay 3 was served by the starboard deck-edge elevator.

Bay 2 was for light work, such as electrical and radio repair, and aircraft storage. The boiler uptakes can be seen along the starboard wall of the bay, which was served by the port deck-edge elevator when that unit was operational.

Bay 1 was used primarily for aircraft storage and was served by the forward flight-deck elevator. Steam accumulators for the catapults are located on both walls; the entrance to the quarterdeck, the official welcoming spot for special visitors, opens onto bay 1.

PLATE 29: FORWARD ELEVATOR

At the forward end of *Lexington*'s hangar deck is the well of No. 1 elevator, the ship's centerline unit, now locked in position on the flight deck. The outline of its shape can be seen between the catapult launch tracks. This is the last of *Lexington*'s original elevators, and was, in fact, the last centerline elevator in operation in the U.S. carrier fleet when *Lexington* was decommissioned in 1991. During World War II, this elevator was 48 feet by 44 feet, with a load capacity of 28,000 pounds. During the ship's 1953–55 modernization, the centerline elevator was enlarged to 70 feet by 44 feet, with a 46,000-pound load limit to handle the larger jet aircraft operated by the navy at that time. On the flight deck, a protective railing surrounded the elevator opening any time the unit was not flush with the deck. A similar railing was positioned around the empty well on the hangar deck when the elevator was up. The unit was secured in the up position during the last years of *Lexington*'s service as a training carrier. The twin pulley assemblies in the foreground and against the lower back wall of the well are part of the hydraulic system for raising and lowering the elevator. The plane is an N3N "Yellow Peril," an early navy trainer. (see aircraft plate A1).

PLATE 30: CONFLAG 3

Each of *Lexington*'s three hangar bays contains a conflagration (CONFLAG) station similar to the one in bay 3, at bottom right. Their primary function was early detection of fire or potential fire and control of fire-fighting efforts on the hangar deck. The hangar decks of U.S. carriers, with unarmored wooden flight decks above them, offered enormous potential for devastating fires when penetrated by bombs. Refueling and rearming of aircraft was carried out on hangar decks, and fuel lines to the aviation gasoline (avgas) tanks were often open or could be ruptured by a bomb blast. Bombs and torpedoes were arriving regularly on the ordnance elevators from the ship's magazines. From the CONFLAG stations, each bay could be closed off by electrically operated fire doors and with fire curtains that sealed openings in the sides of the hangar deck. CONFLAG stations also controlled the overhead sprinklers and the AFFF (Aqueous Film-Forming Foam) stations. CONFLAGS 1 and 3 could operate only the controls for their respective hangar bays, but CONFLAG 2 could control all fire doors and fire-fighting equipment. The walls of the compartment are lined with asbestos, and the observation ports have been reduced to small slits to protect personnel on duty here.

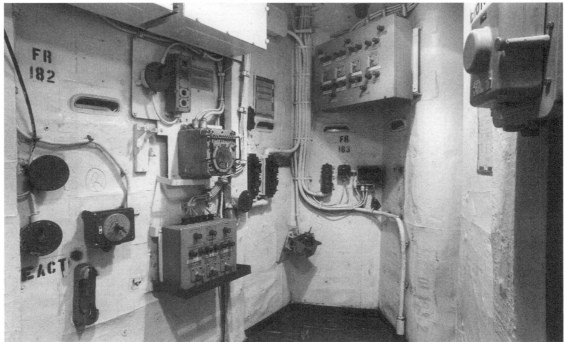

PLATE 31: FIRE-RETARDANT SUIT

A modern flame-retardant suit, worn by a *Lexington* crew member, was on display when Betty Power made this photograph during the ship's 1987 port call in Galveston, Texas. Fire was the gravest threat to aircraft carriers, and much attention was given in design studies to preventing and controlling fire aboard the *Essex*-class carriers.

Carriers contained the source of their own destruction in the aviation gasoline required by their aircraft. The navy's desire for ever-larger air groups aboard *Lexington* and her sister ships led to an increase in fuel storage capacity to more than 230,000 gallons during World War II. Avgas tanks were surrounded by voids and located deep within the armored box of the ships' hulls. Salt water replaced consumed gasoline to prevent spark ignition.

But the avgas tanks had to be opened to refuel aircraft on the hangar decks, beneath the ships' unarmored flight decks. At the Battle of Midway, American pilots reversed the tide of war in the Pacific when their bombs turned the unarmored Japanese carriers *Akagi*, *Kaga*, *Hiryu*, and *Soryu* into towering infernos by igniting open fuel lines.

U.S. carriers had similar experiences. Loss of the first *Lexington* (CV-2) was charged to aviation fuel. Hit by three bombs during the Battle of the Coral Sea, *Lexington* extinguished her fires within ninety minutes, only to be ripped by massive explosions triggered by avgas fumes. The light fleet carrier *Princeton* (CVL-23) suffered a similar fate when a bomb detonated in her hangar, starting fires and knocking out fire-fighting equipment. Two of the *Essex* class, *Franklin* (CV-13) and *Bunker Hill* (CV-17), endured trial by fire but survived; the difference was disciplined damage-control procedures instituted by the navy and improved during the course of the war.

The first—and crucial—step was to make damage control a full-time concern. Prevention became a priority, and each department of the ship was responsible for setting proper material conditions to sustain damage control efforts. Next came organization. Damage control direction was centralized. D.C. Central aboard *Lexington* was located on the port side of the second platform deck, near hull frame 71. Damage control parties were mustered before the ship went into combat, with each party assigned a specific area, such as A section, from the bow to frame 79 below hangar-deck level.

In later years, U.S. carriers benefited from the development of new chemical agents for controlling fires. All eight main machinery spaces on *Lexington* were equipped with the Halon 1301 total flooding system. Halon is a heavier-than-air gas that interrupts the combustion reaction involving oxygen, fuel, and a source of ignition. *Lexington* also deployed the twin-agent system, which used PKP (Purple K Powder) to disrupt oxidation; and either light water, which floated on top of fuel, or AFFF (Aqueous Film-Forming Foam) to seal flammable substances against reignition.

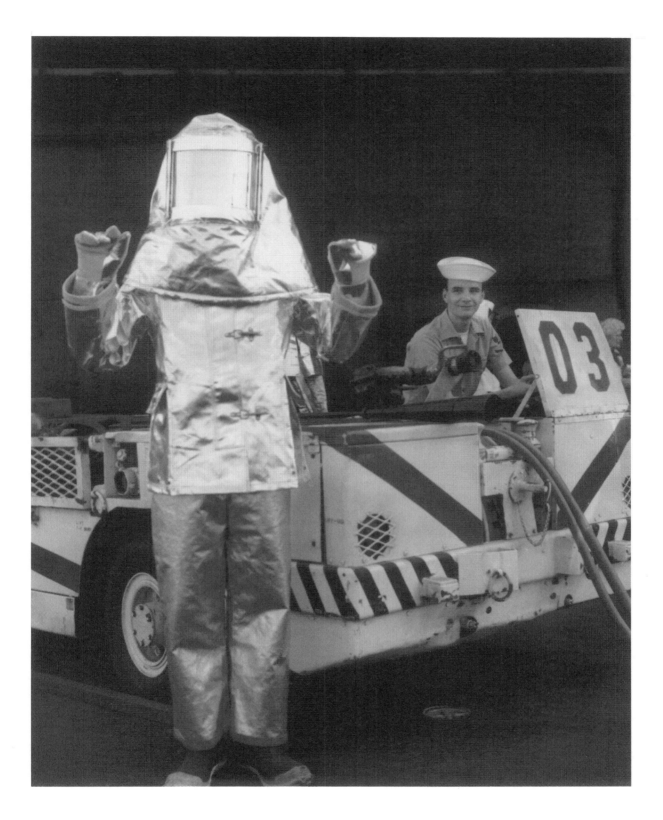

PLATE 32: COMPARTMENTS AND WATERTIGHT DOORS

A hint of *Lexington*'s complexity is evident in this passageway on the starboard side of deck 2. The ship's bulkheads and watertight doors can subdivide it into some four thousand spaces, including void spaces too small for a person but important to ballast and trim. In 1944 the chief of BuShips (Bureau of Ships) reported that the *Essex*es required 9,160 separate construction plans; an *Iowa*-class battleship, the largest ever built by the United States, required only 8,150.

But that complexity was a major key to damage control strategy and the ships' survivability. The maze of internal subdivisions ensured that most flooding could be contained, or at least offset by flooding spaces opposite the battle damage. In judging the success of their damage control design and implementation, it is worth noting that no *Essex*-class carrier was sunk in World War II and that five of the six American carriers lost were sunk in 1942, when carrier damage control was in its infancy.

Indeed, many wartime photographs of *Essex*-class carriers listing after battle damage are deceptive. Often the list was self-induced to allow large volumes of water used in fighting fires—especially on the hangar deck—to run off through openings in the ship's side.

Damage control aboard *Lexington* and her sister ships gains more stature when two major design flaws are acknowledged. Underwater protection against torpedo damage was only slightly improved over the preceding *Yorktown* class, and three of those four ships were lost to torpedoes. More troublesome was a long ventilation trunk, at deck 2 level on the port side, that ran two-thirds the length of the ship. It presented a conduit through which choking smoke and burning gases could penetrate the ship's interior. *Lexington* experienced this when smoke tanks located near the trunk entrance ruptured and toxic clouds spread rapidly throughout the ship. The trunk was omitted from later *Essex*es and removed from earlier ones after 1945.

By war's end, the greater problem for *Lexington* and her sister ships was topside weight. All were top-heavy with new radars, electronic gear, more antiaircraft guns, and from the explosive growth in aircraft size and ordnance loads. One yard inventory revealed that the "ready-use" ammunition stored topside on the *Franklin* (CV-13) weighed 247 tons, about half the total empty weight of the ship's complement of aircraft. And the full load weight of the TBF Avenger, the navy's standard torpedo bomber after 1942, had increased from 13,540 pounds in 1940 to 16,761 pounds in 1945. The heftier topside had produced such a decline in the ships' stability that in 1945 it was estimated some *Essex*es might not survive just two torpedo hits.

PLATE 33: COMBAT INFORMATION CENTER (CIC)

Since World War II, all combat information pathways lead to the combat information center (CIC), located on *Lexington*'s gallery deck. The room is analogous to the human brain but is on-line twenty-four hours a day. The view at right has not been reversed; personnel recording data from behind the plot boards lining one side of the compartment wrote from right to left so that the command staff manning the officer's platform across the room could read the information from left to right.

To oversimplify, CIC collected and evaluated all information on the status of *Lexington*, other friendly ships, and enemy forces, then directed the ship's performance to achieve the assigned mission. In application, that meant many people worked with incredible speed and painstaking cooperation under stress levels utterly unacceptable in civilian life.

The airplane made CIC necessary. As World War II unfolded, warships could no longer concentrate on one target at a time; there were too many of them in the air, and any one might deal a fatal blow. Some central command station was needed to integrate the mass of information coming from lookouts, the ship's own aircraft aloft, other ships in the task force, but mostly from the new radar. Radar was the answer to directing carrier fighter defense, and CIC was the answer to managing the radar.

The concept predated the *Essex*-class ships, but their first CICs still were small, cramped compartments in the island. Very quickly, CICs were moved to roomier quarters on the gallery deck, where *Lexington*'s remains today.

The clear plastic plot boards were CIC's focal point, along with a dead reckoning tracer (DRT) identical to the one in the navigation bridge chart room. There are three vertical, connected plot boards; the first two displayed information on friendly forces, and the third was used for plotting "skunks," which were hostile or unknown contacts. In combat, the plot board at right was a relative plot, with *Lexington* always at its center. The data link reference point (DLRP) then allowed all other vessels or aircraft to be plotted relative to that common position. Personnel recording data on the boards were connected with headsets to their sources of information, from lookouts to the air operations office next door. Other data often came from the electronic warfare/electronic countermeasures (EW/ECM) room located through the entryway at left, behind the desk. The computer at far left in this view is a post–World War II unit that recorded all communications into and out of CIC.

A senior officer—often not an aviator but a surface warfare expert—commanded CIC, assisted by junior officers, phone "talkers," and a force officer representing the task force if an admiral was on board.

PLATE 34: AIR OPERATIONS CENTER AND CATCC

While CIC coordinated combat functions, the air operations (AirOps) office coordinated air traffic to and from *Lexington* and planned upcoming missions. The view at right looks down the duty desk, with the AirOps board at right and the CIC entrance at left. Close coordination was absolutely necessary with CIC, and also with the air officer in Pri-Fly, the flight deck, the hangar deck, the ready rooms, and the carrier air traffic control center (CATCC) next door.

The AirOps board was also plotted from the back side, and personnel wrote backwards as in CIC. The board displayed the daily flight schedule and details, individual aircraft numbers, squadron numbers, operational start and stop times, landing and launch rates and totals, status of the carrier onboard delivery (COD) aircraft, rescue helicopters, and outbound traffic. Information posted under the heading "Bingo" referred to onshore airfields to which aircraft aloft might be diverted for any reason. Fuel requirements to reach Bingo were also posted.

The phone in the middle of the operations desk is red, signifying a secure line on which messages cannot be intercepted. Alongside it are a ship's dial phone, intercom receivers, and 19MC, or "squawk box." Sound-powered phones and radios for direct contact with aircraft line the walls. The map on the desk is an operational navigation chart (ONC). The sheet of plane outlines in the foreground is pure nostalgia, a World War II "Friend or Foe" identification chart, with silhouettes of U.S., British, Japanese, German, and Italian aircraft.

Adjacent to AirOps is CATCC, which functions like an airport approach control radar facility. There were four radar controllers on duty, two each for approach and final approach. Their job was to get planes back on the carrier safely when weather deteriorated and pilots could not make visual contact with the ship.

The process is called carrier-controlled approach (CCA). The approach controllers used the ship's SPN-43 radar to direct, or "vector," the aircraft to the correct altitude, speed, and configuration for landing. Then they turned the pilot over to a final approach controller, who used the more precise SPN-35 radar to guide the pilot until he could see the "meatball" of the optical landing system. The pilot "called the ball" when he made visual contact, and the CATCC controller turned him over to the LSO on the flight deck.

CATCC controllers also directed departing aircraft and aircraft waved off by the LSO and making another approach. Aircraft departing on tactical missions were handed over to CIC. During carrier training in the Gulf of Mexico, *Lexington* coordinated flight operations with Gulf Coast airfields through the FAA Air Route Traffic Control Centers in Houston, Miami, and Jacksonville, Florida.

The recliners are empty, but No. 1 ready room, the largest on board *Lexington*, once was a hub of activity for the ship's pilots. A hint about their significance is that ready rooms were air-conditioned during World War II; pilots delivered the punch that made carriers the dominant naval weapon of 1942–45, and few amenities were spared where air groups were concerned.

Ready rooms served as briefing areas prior to a mission and as squadron "dens," where pilots and air crew could read, nap, or visit while awaiting the order, "Launch planes." No. 1 ready room accommodated all thirty-six pilots in *Lexington*'s fighter squadron during the war, while torpedo and dive-bomber squadrons used similar but smaller compartments. No. 1 was the last ready room in service aboard the ship, used by the helicopter rescue squad during *Lexington*'s last years as a training carrier.

Lexington was designed with four ready rooms, two aft of the midships elevator and two forward of the aft elevator, all on the gallery deck. This placement caused concern, since the unarmored flight decks of *Essex*-class ships left pilots vulnerable in ready rooms immediately below them. In the first postwar modernization, SCB-27A, some ready rooms were moved to protected sites below the armored hangar deck. Under the SCB-27C program, two *Lexington* ready rooms were relocated to lower levels. Since this increased the distance between pilots and planes, escalators to the flight deck were installed. *Lexington*'s escalator is visible on the starboard side, below the island.

As designed, the *Essex*es operated four squadrons of aircraft, one each of fighters, torpedo bombers, dive-bombers, and scout bombers. Even then, it was realized that a carrier's best defensive weapon was its own fighters, and *Lexington* commissioned with a "double squadron" of 36 fighters, plus 18-plane squadrons of each bomber type, totaling 91 operational aircraft plus 9 partially disassembled planes in storage.

By 1944, scout functions had merged with those of the dive-bomber into a single, 24-plane squadron. Yet air-group size kept increasing to accomodate specialty functions, like night-fighting, and the emergence of the fighter-bomber. By *Lexington*'s third war cruise, in 1945, the air group included a fighter squadron of 36 planes, a fighter-bomber squadron the same size, and dive- and torpedo bomber squadrons of 15 planes each, a total of 102 aircraft.

Whatever their numbers and composition, *Lexington*'s air groups performed well. Five groups were assigned to the ship during her World War II combat operations, CVG-16, CVG-19, CVG-20, CVG-9, and CVG-94. Combat air patrols (CAP) and fighter sweeps by those groups shot 387 Japanese planes out of the air; they were even more prolific against Japanese air bases, destroying 635 planes on the ground. Seventeen planes destroyed by the ship's guns brought *Lexington*'s total to 1,039 Japanese aircraft destroyed. The air groups also hit hard at Japanese surface ships, both military and merchant. CVG-19 was the undisputed leader, claiming 267,000 tons of naval and 148,000 tons of merchant shipping sunk or damaged. Overall, *Lexington*'s planes sank or damaged 77 ships totaling 1,085,000 tons.

PLATE 36: FOC'SLE ANCHOR CONTROL STATION

Lexington carried two anchors through her forty-eight-year career, both mounted in the bow and controlled from this station in the forecastle, or foc'sle. The wheel in the foreground is the hoist-and-lower control; behind it is the brake control wheel. The anchor chain can be seen at upper left, running around the circular bronze drum of the wildcat brake and then to the chain pipe behind the white stanchions and into the chain locker.

Lexington's anchors weigh more than 15 tons each and are designated Bertha, attached at the starboard bow; and Brutus, the portside anchor, at the foot of the pier leading to the ship. Each anchor chain link weighs 112–30 pounds. The foc'sle is the primary work station of the "boatswain mates" (bosuns), who operate and maintain the equipment. The foc'sle forward of the collision bulkhead was open during World War II and was then enclosed in the hurricane bow during the 1953–55 modernization.

The geared wildcats are run by windlass motors located below the foc'sle deck. The chains run from the wildcats to hawse pipes in the "bullnose," the ship's forwardmost compartment, where they attach to the anchor ring. Attached along that stretch of chain are stoppers, which are short lengths of chain used to relieve strain on the wildcat and secure the anchor chain to the deck. The stoppers are attached to a deck cleat, then to the chain with a pelican hook, bale shackle, and bale shackle pin. A turnbuckle adjusts tension on the stoppers, and the oversized wrenches on the stanchions were used to adjust the turnbuckles.

Anchoring was a complex maneuver that required precise coordination between the bridge and foc'sle. Three separate command systems, all originating on the bridge, were used to order the anchor raised or lowered. The first order came through the annunciator, located on the foc'sle collision bulkhead. A second command was sent by bell, and final confirmation came by phone.

On the first order, the bale shackle pin was removed and the wildcat brake set. At the final command, "Let go the anchor," the bail shackle was knocked off with a maul and the pelican hook opened, releasing the chain. The brake spun wildly—hence, the name "wildcat"—as the anchor descended. The length of chain used to anchor is usually six times the depth of the water, more if foul weather is anticipated. When getting under way, the anchor was hoisted by the wildcat and washed down as it cleared the water. The anchors were used interchangeably, based on the situation, though the starboard anchor was used most often, since it could be seen more easily from the bridge.

The capstans, located adjacent to the wildcats, also operated off the windlass motors and controlled the lines used for mooring to a pier. For towing, the port anchor was detached from the wildcat, and the chain was run out through the center of the bullnose.

PLATES 37 AND 38: CAPTAIN'S STATEROOM AND GALLEY

While captains of U.S. capital ships—carriers and battleships—lived in their day cabins at sea, they could look forward to more amenable quarters in port, like the comfortable suite of rooms located on *Lexington*'s gallery deck. Larger than during World War II, the suite includes a stateroom (bedroom), top, bathroom, walk-in closet, large sitting room, dining area, and stainless steel galley, bottom. A polished silver eagle identifying his rank is embedded in the deck at the entrance to the captain's quarters.

The suite includes a classified vault, lined with shelves for storage of confidential publications, reports, maps, and messages. An outside entry that resembles a bank vault door with a combination lock opens into a passageway.

During World War II, the captain's in-port quarters were one of the few air-conditioned spaces on the ship, though the air-conditioning was crude and often out of commission. The area was not carpeted at that time and had no padded furniture like the chair in the upper photograph. The round escape hatch against the back wall of the bedroom opens onto an external walkaround.

The captain's quarters were served by two professional stewards, enlisted "regulars" in the United States Navy. Usually African-American or Filipino, their sole task was to attend to the captain's needs—cleaning his quarters, cooking his meals, and doing his laundry. Filipinos who served as stewards became United States citizens at the end of their enlistment period.

If the captain's quarters seem incongruous with the purpose of a warship, it should be remembered that U.S. Navy vessels often conduct diplomacy by "showing the flag" in foreign ports, where the captain becomes a combination host and goodwill ambassador. In fact, in countries where there is no U.S. ambassador, the captains of navy ships have often filled that void. Entertaining dignitaries was also a common occurrence aboard large warships. The secretary of the navy can always stay the night aboard a U.S. Navy vessel. And among the entertainment celebrities who have graced *Lexington* are Elizabeth Taylor, Bob Hope, Sammy Davis, Jr., and Brooke Shields.

Since *Lexington*'s recommissioning in 1955, twenty-nine men have served as captain. The first of these was Alexander S. Heyward, Jr., from August of 1955 to October of 1956. The longest continuous stretch of service was that of C. Flack Logan, who commanded the ship for thirty-one months, from May of 1988 to December of 1990. One captain, Jack E. Davis, commanded the ship twice, from April of 1971 to December of 1972, and again from August to November of 1973. The ship's last captain was William Kennedy, who served from December of 1990 to decommissioning in November of 1991.

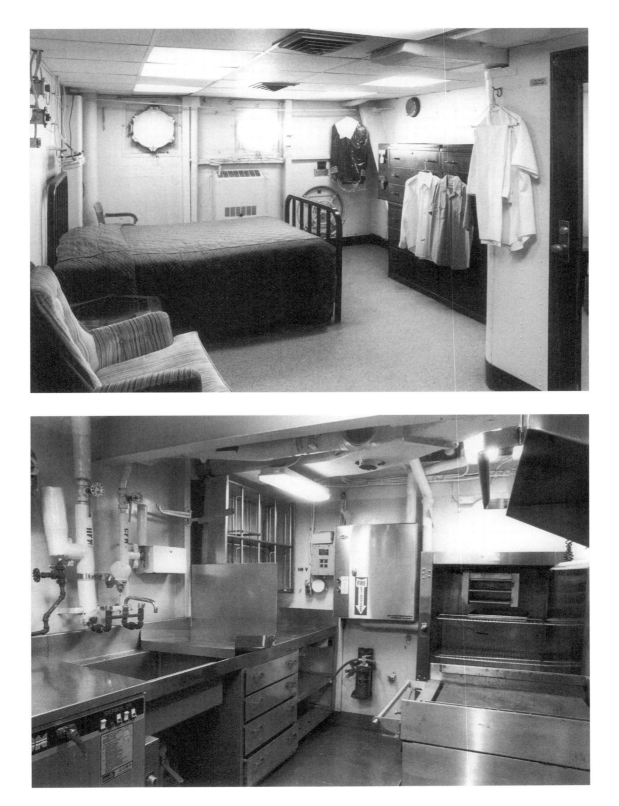

PLATE 39: ADMIRAL'S CABIN

All *Essex*-class carriers were designed to function as flagships, and *Lexington* spent more time in that role during World War II than most of her sister ships. Like the bridges, the admiral's in-port quarters are adjacent to those of the captain, just across a passageway on the gallery deck. The suite includes a bedroom, bathroom, walk-in closet, cabin (sitting room), top, dining room, and stainless steel galley. The cabin was used for conferences and entertaining VIPs; today it contains books, photos, and other memorabilia collected by *Lexington* veterans. Tradition has it that the color scheme of the table and chair coverings in the cabin indicated the purpose of an upcoming meeting. White was for dining; blue was for meetings; and green was for a mast, convened to determine punishment of a crew member. A chief and steward oversaw the purchasing and preparation of food for the admiral's galley, and they were always in attendance when their flag officer was aboard. The length of time he was to be on board and the size force he commanded determined what size staff an admiral brought with him. Quarters for his chief of staff were located in the next room aft from the admiral's quarters. Admirals, like captains, stayed close to their posts when at sea, and there is a sea cabin for the flag officer on the 05 level in the island, just aft of the tactical plot room on the flag bridge.

PLATE 40: JUNIOR OFFICERS' QUARTERS

The junior officers' quarters are located on the 01 level in the *Lexington*'s forecastle, usually written "foc'sle" and pronounced "folks'l." The name originated in the days of sailing ships, when castle-like structures were located forward and above the main deck. Junior officers' quarters on *Lexington* were occupied primarily by ensigns, the lowest commissioned rank in the navy, or by junior officers on temporary assignment, earning this area the nickname "Boys' Town." During *Lexington*'s training carrier career, this area was used by air group personnel undergoing carrier qualifications. Each "alley" contained six "racks," or bunks; what appear to be tissue boxes actually held emergency breathing apparatus. At the far end of the bunkroom is the junior officers' lounge, which includes a display of the game board for "Acey Ducey," a form of backgammon and a traditional navy favorite. Individual staterooms elsewhere in the foc'sle were assigned to commanders, department heads, and squadron leaders. These senior officers' quarters contained a bed, dresser, desk, bookcase, locker, small safe, and wash basin, and they were also used as offices. Lieutenant commanders and lieutenants shared staterooms, and lieutenants j.g. (junior grade) bunked four to a room. Enlisted personnel quarters were similar to the junior officers' bunkroom but were more crowded and lacked desks. Enlisted berthing was scattered throughout the ship, including some areas of the foc'sle.

The quality of navy food is traditionally best aboard large warships, and since World War II, aircraft carriers have been regarded as the best duty a sailor can draw for cuisine. The diet aboard *Lexington* was very good, and the ship often won awards for food service. Officers ate in the wardroom, at top right, while enlisted personnel were served cafeteria-style in the enlisted mess, bottom right, located today on deck 3.

During World War II, when *Lexington*'s crew swelled to more than three thousand, messing began at 0500 (5 A.M.) and continued until 2230 (10:30 P.M.). Most carriers assigned a special mess to the air department. Because of that department's odd operational schedule, it often took four hours to feed the air personnel, compared to about a hundred minutes for other departments. When the ship was at general quarters, cooks prepared soup and sandwiches, and mess stewards delivered them to the men at their duty stations. Among the large commissary staff, bakers were unquestionably the most popular and were treated by everyone with special care.

A typical wardroom mess schedule for *Lexington* at sea during the ship's training career called for breakfast at 0800 hours; lunch cafeteria-style from 1100 to 1230; dinner from 1700 to 1730 for watchstanders only, followed by sit-down service—"family style"—at 1800 for all other officers. Late service was from 1845 to half an hour after flight quarters and at 2300 for "midrats," officers standing the midwatch from 2400 to 0400. A typical in-port wardroom schedule served breakfast at 0730 hours, lunch cafeteria-style from 1130 to 1230, and a sit-down dinner at 1730. The decorative rope patterns on the support stanchions in the wardroom are called "fancy work," and are done by the bosuns.

The enlisted personnel cafeteria served hot meals on the side shown here, while the other side served fast food. A typical menu, taken from an August, 1961, issue of the *Sunrise Press*, the ship's newspaper, listed morning meal selections of chilled fresh fruit, dry cereal, eggs, French or hot toast, sausage, bacon, pastries, milk, coffee, and juice.

The noon menu included clam chowder, fried shrimp, sea bass, veal stew, au gratin potatoes, a salad bar, banana layer cake, milk, and coffee. The evening menu offered tomato barley soup, roast beef, ham, sweet potatoes, asparagus, apple pie à la mode, milk, and coffee. Daily food consumption was prodigious, averaging 660 pounds of meat, 164 gallons of milk, and 97 dozen eggs. One steak meal required 850 pounds of beef.

The mess deck also featured a "Geedunk Stand," or soda fountain, that served candy, soft drinks, and ice cream. The ship's store, on deck 2, offered toiletries and tobacco products.

PLATE 43: HEAD

There are more than a hundred washrooms like the one shown here aboard *Lexington*. Called heads in navy jargon, they contain hundreds of toilets, wash basins, and showers made of stainless steel, which is easy to clean and sanitize. Latrine duty was a daily event, and shower stalls were scrubbed down weekly. Sometimes containing only a single toilet, heads are located in unexpected nooks and crannies around the ship, reflecting the navy's concern that toilets be within easy reach of all personnel to minimize time away from their posts during combat operations. Yet even *Lexington*'s facilities were strained when the ship transported ground troops to Hawaii during World War II. On those trips, open toilet troughs were fitted on the fantail, with continuous running water flushing waste into the sea. Pranksters would set fire to rolls of toilet paper at one end of the trough and float them to the opposite end, giving new meaning to the term "hot seat." Human waste from *Lexington*'s crew went into CHT (collection and holding tanks), where it was liquified by large blades. When the CHT tanks filled, pumps automatically emptied them into the ocean. A total of 180,000 gallons of fresh water—about 12.5 gallons per person for *Lexington*'s 1991 crew of 1,443—was produced each day by the ship's four evaporators, which also supplied feed water to the boilers. Fresh water was stored in tanks positioned throughout the ship.

PLATE 44: BARBER SHOP

Lexington's barber shop has been relocated since World War II and is found today on deck 2, just forward of the medical complex. Enlisted men were served in the room shown at right, which contains four chairs. Officers used a smaller, one-chair shop adjacent to this one. Trained barbers were selected from the crew and held the rank of ordinary seaman barber, working under a chief barber. In both navy and civilian life, some rules are universal; the better a seaman was known to tip, the faster he got served. During World War II, the navy's concerns over hair length were specific enough to merit this entry in the 1943 *Bluejacket's Manual*: "The hair, beard and mustache must be worn neatly trimmed. The face must be kept clean-shaved, except a mustache or beard and mustache may be worn at discretion. No eccentricities in the manner of wearing the hair, beard or mustache are allowed." And none were. At that time, crew members paid a twenty-five-cent chit—a ship's token—for a shave and haircut of regulation length. This was a requirement for "liberty," the privilege of going ashore when *Lexington* was in port. Regulations have relaxed somewhat in the intervening years, and goatees and more creative mustaches are tolerated today, though neatness still counts with a crew member's immediate superior. Reflected in the mirror is a detailed graffiti study, one of several such displays that adorn *Lexington*'s bulkheads. This one was copied by crew members from magazine work by the caricaturist Frank Caruso.

PLATE 45: ENGINE LATHE

Aircraft carriers may be the most self-sufficient warships built by the United States Navy; this quality was a critical prerequisite for long periods of operation over the vast reaches of the Pacific during World War II. Usually far removed from land-based repair facilities, carriers could not break down from daily wear and tear, necessitating a trip home every few days or weeks, and be the dominant arbitors of American victory over the Japanese. Instead, they had to be able to repair themselves.

Since the beginnings of steam power in the nineteenth century, large warships have been equipped with on-board repair facilities, but nothing as extensive as those aboard aircraft carriers. *Lexington*'s machine shop is a classic example. Located on deck 3, it contains 1,240 square feet of operating space. Two bulkheads have been removed to allow visitors a better look at the shop's extensive array of equipment.

Using that equipment, the ship's complement of six to eight machinery repairmen (MRs) were able to solve breakdown problems throughout the ship, often fabricating new parts to replace worn out ones. Overhead tracks entering the machine shop from adjacent passageways facilitated movement of heavy pieces. Machinery like the engine lathe shown at right is still in operating order today and used by the *Lexington*'s staff to carry out repairs aboard the museum.

The shop contains five engine lathes, one of which is from the ship's original World War II complement of equipment. Other machinery from 1942 includes a vertical milling machine, pedestal grinder, and a radial arm drill press.

The shop also contains a horizontal milling machine, a dynamic balancing machine, a bench grinder, a drill press, a power hacksaw, and a pantograph. Most of the pieces and all four original World War II units have been updated with digital controls, and some of the latest equipment was installed as recently as 1987. The most modern engine lathes date from 1983 and 1984.

PLATES 46 AND 47: SURGICAL DRESSING STATION AND SICK BAY

During World War II, large warships were expected to meet their own medical needs, and those of smaller warships as well. From her design stage, *Lexington* has maintained a sick bay the size of a well-equipped small-town hospital. The facility had forty-nine beds during the war and was served by a staff of three flight surgeons, two administrative officers, and thirty hospital corpsmen. Relocated from deck 3 to deck 2 after the war, sick bay had twenty beds and state-of-the-art equipment during *Lexington*'s tenure as a training carrier. Peace-time staff consisted of two flight surgeons, fourteen corpsmen, two dentists, and seven dental technicians.

The top view shows the emergency treatment, or triage, room, and at bottom is a portion of the twenty-bed ward. The triage room is adjacent to the main operating room, and a smaller compartment between them contained autoclaves for sterilizing instruments. Everything from minor cuts to major non-invasive treatments were handled in triage, which could also be used for full-scale surgical procedures.

The ward housed patients unable to return immediately to duty, and treatment rooms in the sick bay complex could be used as isolation units for contagious disease cases. The ward had its own head, with showers and whirlpool bath, and each bunk was equipped with a lamp and breathing apparatus. During World War II, crew space was used to expand sick bay, especially after the kamikaze hit of November 5, 1944, which wounded 132 crew members.

If some equipment looks new, it probably is. Sick bay was upgraded every three years. The main operating table is less than a decade old; and the X-ray machine, called a picker unit, is of 1986 vintage. The picker unit shot some 3,700 X-rays monthly, and its lead-lined room was also used to identify the remains of accident victims. A unique piece of heavy equipment is the hearing test chamber. The closed booth is sound-proof, and patients inside could be tested for hearing loss. Such tests were run regularly on pilots and engine room, and flight deck personnel, who were the crew members most exposed to high levels of noise.

The sick call station was the hub of the medical department, where hospital corpsmen and physicians examined crew members, made diagnoses, prescribed treatment, and made referrals to other areas of sick bay.

Sick bay also includes a lab for diagnostic testing; ophthalmic equipment to diagnose vision problems; a preventive medicine section that set environmental health standards for the ship; an administrative and medical records section for maintaining patient histories; and a pharmacy that stocked some twelve hundred items.

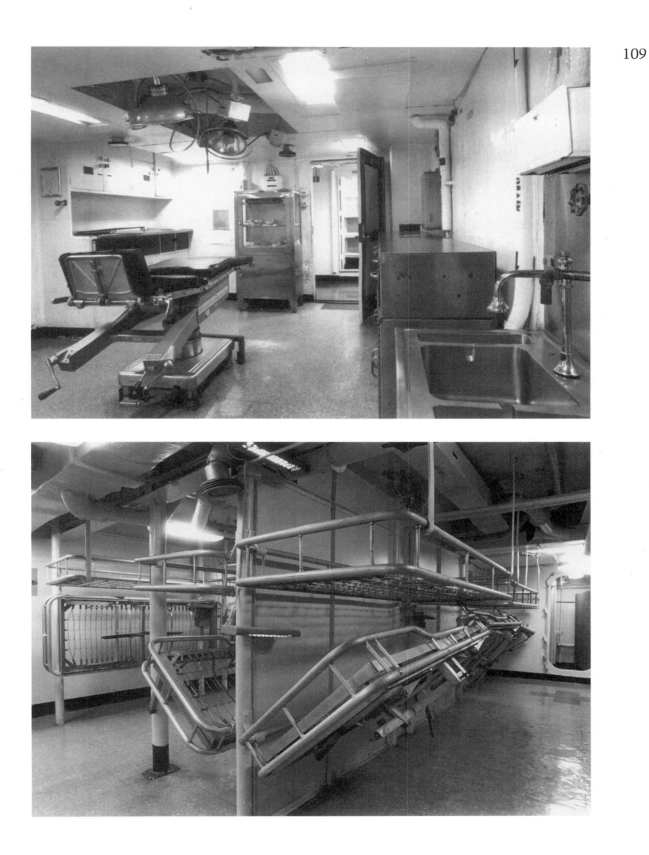

PLATES 48 AND 49: ENGINE ROOM
CONTROL STATION AND TURBINE DETAIL

The *Lexington* and her sister ships were powered by one of the most efficient and dependable propulsion systems ever installed in United States Navy warships. The power plant consisted of four Westinghouse geared turbine engines, fired by eight Babcock & Wilcox boilers. This system developed 150,000 horsepower, a top ahead speed of 33 knots, and a backing speed of 20 knots. The top view is the control station for one of two cross-compound turbine engines in the after engine room. The bottom view details the arrangement of the high-pressure and low-pressure turbines that constitute each engine.

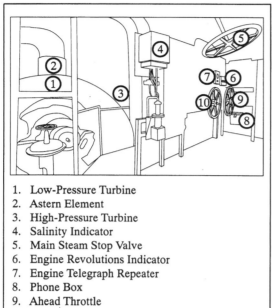

1. Low-Pressure Turbine
2. Astern Element
3. High-Pressure Turbine
4. Salinity Indicator
5. Main Steam Stop Valve
6. Engine Revolutions Indicator
7. Engine Telegraph Repeater
8. Phone Box
9. Ahead Throttle
10. Astern Throttle

During preliminary design of the *Essex* class, engines were a major source of debate. The navy wanted high astern speed in order to land aircraft over the bow in case battle damage made the after flight deck unusable. But high-speed backing damaged turbine blades, so turbo-electric and electric drive alternatives were considered. Both consumed too much internal space, creating damage control problems. Instead, the Navy General Board chose a handy alternative, the geared turbine plant already being used in *Atlanta*-class cruisers.

Turbine engines are relatively simple, with a closed-loop system of water and steam accounting for much of their efficiency. Purified water was heated in the boilers, producing saturated steam to drive auxiliary machinery and superheated dry steam. The dry steam, with pressure of 600 pounds per square inch (psi) at 850 degrees Fahrenheit, was piped into the high-pressure turbine, where it expanded through circular rows of blades. It then crossed over through a connecting duct into the center of the low-pressure turbine, where it expanded in both directions to balance the thrust. In both turbines, the revolving blades turned a shaft at up to 1,600 revolutions per minute (rpms). The shafts of both turbines are connected to the main propeller shaft through locked train, double reduction gears that reduce the high rpms to the lower revolutions that equate to the speeds of a ship. Exhausted steam was collected in a main condenser under the low-pressure turbine and recycled through the system.

Each low-pressure turbine on *Lexington* is fitted with an astern element, shown in the bottom view at right, which contains "backing blades" to which steam was diverted when backing the engines. This met the navy's requirement for an astern speed of 20 knots. The machinery spaces were arranged within the hull for maximum resistance to battle damage: each pair of boiler rooms was followed by an engine room. The forward engine room drove the outer propeller shafts, Nos. 1 and 4, while the after engine room drove the inner shafts, Nos. 2 and 3.

PLATES 50 AND 51: BOILER ROOM AND MAIN DISTRIBUTION BOARD

Even in the nuclear age, steam—the stuff of teakettles, but much hotter—still propels navy warships. The efficiency of their steam plant, designed around a closed-loop system, made the *Essex*-class reliable ships and contributed heavily to *Lexington*'s record as the longest-serving carrier in U.S. Navy history.

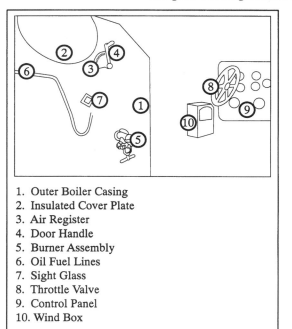

1. Outer Boiler Casing
2. Insulated Cover Plate
3. Air Register
4. Door Handle
5. Burner Assembly
6. Oil Fuel Lines
7. Sight Glass
8. Throttle Valve
9. Control Panel
10. Wind Box

That plant consisted of eight Babcock & Wilcox M-type boilers, like the one at top right in *Lexington*'s No. 4 fireroom. The boilers burned fuel oil, as thick as molasses, in order to turn sea water into steam, which ran engines that were marvels of precision in their time. The sea water was first purged of salt and other impurities in four evaporators, then passed to deaerating feed tanks (DFTs) in the ship's engine rooms. DFTs acted as reservoirs, removed air and noncondensable gases from the water, and preheated it to 250 degrees at a pressure of 17 psi.

The feed water was then pumped through the boilers, where it was converted to dry steam superheated to 850 degrees and 600 psi by fires that consumed 28,000 gallons of No. 6 fuel oil per hour when the *Lexington* was at flank speed. The steam flowed from the boiler rooms to the high-pressure turbines in the engine rooms, crossed over into the low-pressure turbines, and was then collected and condensed back to water in the main condensers and returned to the DFTs to begin the cycle again. Two boilers fed each of four engines, and boilers and engines could be cross-connected should any unit malfunction or suffer damage. The boilers also produced saturated steam that was used to run auxiliary equipment and provide heating for living spaces.

The major auxiliary system that depended on steam was the ship's electrical plant. Control and monitoring of *Lexington*'s electrical power was handled by four switchboards like the one at bottom right in *Lexington*'s No. 4 boiler room. Power was generated by four 1250kW turbo generators, located in the forward auxiliary machinery room, No. 1 engine room, and Nos. 3 and 4 boiler rooms. Two 250kW diesel generators were available, one in each auxiliary machinery room, to compensate for any loss of steam to the turbo generators. That plant provided 5500kW of electricity for *Lexington* during World War II. The diesel generators were upgraded to two 1,000kW units during the SCB-27C modernization, giving the ship a total of 7,000kW. To put that in perspective, the first *Lexington* (CV-2) carried four turbo generators that produced 4500kW, and in 1929 that ship supplied electrical power for the city of Tacoma, Washington, when low rivers shut down the city's main power plant.

USS *Lexington*, last World War II aircraft carrier to decommission from the United States Navy, rests at her final anchorage in Corpus Christi, Texas, with her bow to the sea in this aerial view by Jim Cruz. *Lexington* was decommissioned on November 8, 1991, at Pensacola, Florida, Naval Air Station, her home port since 1962. On January 23, 1992, the ship was awarded to the Corpus Christi Area Convention and Visitors Bureau by Sec. of the Navy H. Lawrence Garrett.

The retirement was inevitable. Aging machinery and systems were costing more each year, in a shrinking military budget. In August of 1990, the secretary of the navy announced that *Lexington* would be replaced at Pensacola by USS *Forrestal* (CVA-59), a ship more than twelve years younger. *Lexington* recorded her final landing on March 8, 1991, when Lt. Kathleen Owens, USN, flew a perfect trap on No. 3 arresting wire. After that, the ship was to be scrapped unless a suitable alternative could be found.

Five cities, including Corpus Christi and Pensacola, began planning efforts to acquire *Lexington* as a naval aviation museum. Also in the running were Mobile, Alabama, already home to the World War II battleship USS *Alabama* (BB-60); Quincy, Massachusetts, where *Lexington* was constructed; and Miami.

But Corpus Christi's campaign won the ship, in no small part because the Corpus Christi City Council voted a $3 million bond sale to support the effort and finance the physical preparations to accomodate the ship. Those preparations were extensive.

First, a sixteen-foot deep "anchorage" was dredged adjacent to the north shore of Corpus Christi, near the entrance to the port, at upper right in this aerial view. A channel was dredged to the anchorage from the deepened passage through Corpus Christi Bay taken by oceangoing vessels and barges like the one crossing *Lexington*'s bow here.

The carrier was towed from Pensacola to Naval Station Ingleside, north of Corpus Christi, and on March 13, 1992, Pres. George Bush transferred the ship to the Corpus Christi ACVB. *Lexington* was towed to her final berth on June 17, 1992, positioned over her new anchorage, and "sunk" into it by pumping fuel and ballast tanks full of water specially treated to prevent internal deterioration. An underwater levee was dredged up around the ship's hull to ensure stability and protection against hurricanes; it will take a tidal surge of more than fifteen feet to float *Lexington* off the bottom.

In addition, a cathodic hull protection system was installed, with anodes placed around and out from the hull. A low-level electric current that passes through them attracts rust away from the hull and to the replaceable anodes instead.

Clean-up activity, safety inspections, and tourism marketing followed. On October 14, 1992, just five months after the ship was turned over by the navy, the USS *Lexington* Museum on the Bay opened to visitors. There were nearly half a million the first year, which was well ahead of attendance and revenue projections.

Lexington joins sister ships *Intrepid* (CV-11), in New York Harbor, and the second *Yorktown* (CV-10), at Charleston, South

Carolina, as a museum and monument to what were, perhaps, the most successful warships ever built by the United States Navy. Yet *Lexington* remains special; the first *Lexington* (CV-2) was the first U.S. carrier lost in war. The second *Lexington* was the last to decommission of the carriers that fought and won that war. In her own history and in the reverence for her predecessor evident in the ship's exhibits, USS *Lexington* may be the most fitting memorial to the history of naval aviation.

PLATES OF AIRCRAFT

All aircraft pictured in this section are on loan from the National Museum of Naval Aviation at Pensacola, Florida, to the USS *Lexington* Museum on the Bay in Corpus Christi, Texas. Text accompanying the aircraft photographs is reprinted courtesy of the USS *Lexington* Museum on the Bay.

PLATE A1: N3N YELLOW PERIL

Wingspan: 34 ft.
Length: 25 ft. 6 in.
Height: 10 ft. 10 in.
Weight: 2,792 lbs.
Power Plant: One 235-hp Wright R-760-2 engine.
Speed: 126 mph maximum, 90 mph cruising.
Range: 470 miles.
Ceiling: 15,200 ft.
Manufacturer: Naval Aircraft Factory.

In 1934 the U.S. Navy developed a new primary trainer with a steel-tube fuselage and wing construction covered with fabric. The plane was widely used as a primary trainer in the late 1930s and 1940s, and it was known as the Yellow Peril by the thousands of naval aviators who trained in it. Upon completion of primary flight training in the N3N, pilots transferred to more powerful and sophisticated aircraft. Most N3Ns were declared surplus after World War II. Many were purchased by civilians, fitted with more powerful engines, and used as crop dusters. As a result, many are still flying today.

PLATE A2: GH-3 NIGHTINGALE

Wingspan: 38 ft.
Length: 25 ft. 8 in.
Weight: 4,350 lbs.
Power Plant: One Pratt & Whitney R-985 engine.
Speed: 201 mph maximum.
Manufacturer: Howard Corporation.

Based on the Howard Corporation's prewar DGA—an acronym for Damn Good Plane—the GH series was produced in quantity for navy use from 1941 onward. It was employed as a utility aircraft carrying passengers and cargo and as an instrument trainer.

PLATE A3: SNJ TEXAN

Wingspan: 42 ft. 14 in.
Length: 29 ft. 6 in.
Height: 11 ft. 8 1/2 in.
Weight: 5,300 lbs.
Power Plant: One 550-hp Pratt & Whitney R-1340-AN-1 engine.
Armament: Two forward-firing .30-caliber machine guns.
Speed: 205 mph maximum, 170 mph cruising.
Range: 750 miles.
Ceiling: 21,500 ft.
Manufacturer: North American Aviation.

The Texan was the navy's advanced trainer aircraft from 1936 through the 1940s and a primary trainer in the 1950s. It is generally considered the most successful training aircraft ever designed and was used extensively by the navy and air force, as well as by many foreign countries. The navy's SNJ featured a provision for armament, and many were fitted with tailhooks for carrier-landing training. On April 22, 1943, an SNJ-4C piloted by Air Officer Bennet Wright made the first landing on *Lexington* while the ship was undergoing sea trials off the New England coast. The mannequin here is dressed in typical World War II navy flying gear. Note the clipboard attached at the right knee and the inflatable "Mae West" life jacket.

PLATE A4: PV-2D HARPOON

Wingspan: 74 ft. 11 in.
Length: 52 ft.
Height: 11 ft. 11 in.
Weight: 36,000 lbs.
Power Plant: Two 2,000-hp Pratt & Whitney R-2800-31 engines.
Armament: Varied; generally 6–8 Browning .30-caliber or .50-caliber machine guns. Bombload was 2,500 lbs.
Speed: 282 mph maximum, 171 mph cruising.
Range: 1,700 miles.
Ceiling: 23,900 ft.
Manufacturer: Lockheed Aircraft Corporation.

Though never based on carriers, the Harpoon nevertheless played a vital role for the navy during World War II. In early 1942, as the vulnerability of flying boats to Japanese fighters became more apparent the navy began to use land-based patrol bombers. The PV-2 developed for that role was a longer-ranged version of the Army Air Force's PV-1. After serving primarily in the Pacific during the final years of the war, Harpoons were withdrawn from frontline service, but they continued in use with U.S. Navy Reserve wings for several years. Note the closely clustered machine gun battery under the nose of the Harpoon on board *Lexington*.

PLATES A5 AND A6: TBF / TBM-3 AVENGER

Wingspan: 54 ft. 2 in.
Length: 40 ft.
Height: 16 ft. 5 in.
Weight: 10,843 lbs. empty, 18,250 lbs. maximum.
Power Plant: One 1,900-hp Wright R-2600-20 engine.
Armament: Two fixed forward-firing .50-caliber machine guns; one .30-caliber machine gun in ventral position; one .50-caliber machine gun in Grumman 150SE power turret in dorsal position; one Mark 13 torpedo or 2,000 lbs. of bombs; depth charges and/or rockets could be carried externally.
Speed: 267 mph maximum.
Range: 1,130 miles.
Ceiling: 23,400 ft.
Crew: Three: pilot, bombardier/radio operator, and gunner.
Manufacturer: Grumman and Eastern Aircraft.

The first prototype of the Grumman TBF was lost when an in-flight fire forced the test pilot and engineer to bail out. The second prototype made its first flight on December 15, 1941; coming just a week after the Japanese attack on Pearl Harbor, it was christened the Avenger.

The first production TBF rolled off the assembly line on January 3, 1942, and within eight months all carrier-based torpedo squadrons were reequipped with TBFs. The Avenger replaced the obsolete Douglas TBD-1 Devastators, which had performed poorly and suffered horrendous losses at the Battle of Midway in June of 1942.

The wings of the Avenger were designed to fold back laterally along the fuselage, to alleviate the height problem caused on carrier hangar decks by upward-folding wings. The hydraulically powered wings could be folded or unfolded by the pilot in seconds and required no assistance from hangar-deck crews.

Eastern Aircraft, then a division of General Motors, produced the TBMs, and Grumman built the TBFs, but the planes were virtually identical. The record month for TBM production was March, 1945, when Eastern built four hundred aircraft in thirty days.

Avengers became the navy's standard and most effective torpedo bomber during World War II, but it could deliver other payloads as well. Armed with depth charges in the Atlantic, Avengers played a key role in the hunter-killer groups that defeated Germany's U-boats. In the Pacific, Avengers struck targets on both land and sea, and they counted among their pilots former president George Bush. Teamed with dive-bombers, Avengers helped sink the world's largest battleships, the seventy-thousand-ton Japanese *Yamato*s. Avengers scored eleven torpedo hits on the *Musashi* at the Battle of Leyte Gulf on October 24, 1944, and thirteen hits on *Yamato* off Okinawa on April 7, 1945. Avengers were the only torpedo bombers to operate from *Lexington*, and the Avenger at the main visitor entrance is the TBF version.

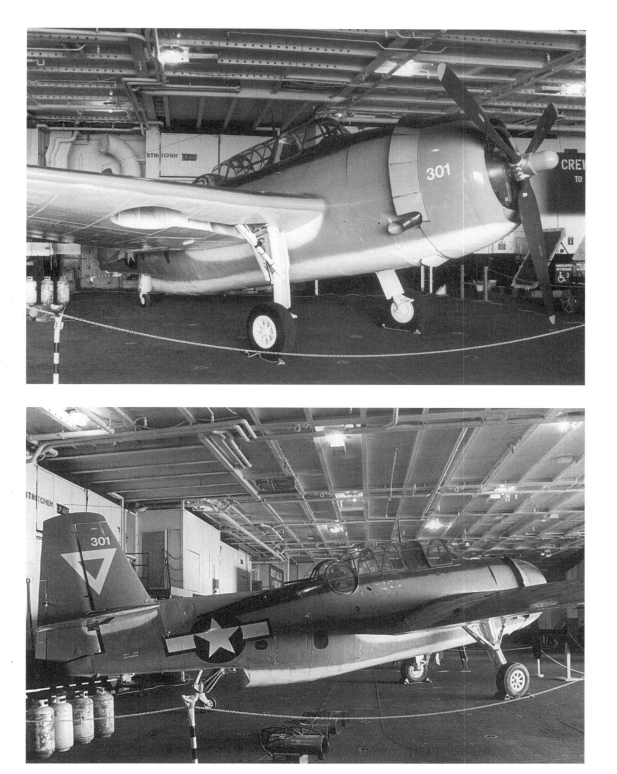

PLATE A7: F2H-2 BANSHEE

Wingspan: 44 ft. 10 in.
Length: 40 ft. 2 in.
Height: 14 ft. 6 in.
Weight: 22,312 lbs.
Power Plant: Two
3,250-lb. thrust
Westinghouse
J34-WE-34 turbojets.
Armament: Four 20mm
cannon and two
500-lb. bombs.
Speed: 532 mph
maximum, 501 mph
cruising.
Range: 1,475 miles.
Ceiling: 44,800 ft.
Manufacturer: McDonnell Aircraft Company.

The Banshee was a second-generation navy jet that basically upgraded the technology of the FH-1 Phantom. It represented a relatively safe approach to increased performance, and many of its specifications are nearly twice those of the Phantom. The F2H was a stable, reliable aircraft that performed well in the shipboard environment. Banshee pilots affectionately nicknamed the plane "Banjo." After *Lexington*'s recommissioning in August of 1955, Banshees flown by Squadron VF-52, Air Task Group 1, operated off the ship during her deployment in the Western Pacific from May 28 to December 20, 1956.

PLATE A8: F9F-8 COUGAR

Wingspan: 34 ft. 6 in.
Length: 44 ft. 5 in.
Height: 12 ft. 3 in.
Weight: 20,600 lbs.
Power Plant: One
7,200-lb. thrust Pratt
& Whitney turbojet.
Armament: Two
forward-firing
machine guns.
Speed: 705 mph
maximum.
Range: 600 miles.
Ceiling: 50,000 ft.
Manufacturer: Grumman Aircraft Engineering Company.

The F9F-6 was the first swept-wing version of the F9F series, taking to the skies in September, 1951. It evolved into the F9F-8/8T, the last in a long line of F9F-series fighters built for the navy by Grumman. The F9F-8, first flown in December, 1953, had a large fuel capacity and a slightly different wing and canopy than its predecessors. More than seven hundred of the aircraft were built, and at one time, they provided the majority of the navy's fighter strength. The last 8Ts were retired in February, 1974. Cougars were also the first swept-wing aircraft used by the navy's precision flying team, the Blue Angels, who flew the F9F-8 from 1955 to 1957. The Cougar aboard *Lexington* has been refurbished by the ship's restoration team to display the paint scheme and insignia of the Blue Angels.

PLATE A9: A3D SKYWARRIOR

Wingspan: 72 ft. 6 in.
Length: 76 ft. 4 in.
Height: 22 ft. 10 in.
Weight: 82,000 lbs.
Power Plant: Two 12,400-lb. thrust Pratt & Whitney J57-P-10 turbojets.
Armament: Two remote-controlled 20mm cannon in tail turret and a bomb load of 12,000 lbs.
Speed: 610 mph maximum.
Range: 2,000 miles.
Ceiling: 43,000 ft.
Manufacturer: Douglas Aircraft Company.

The Skywarrior evolved from a 1947 navy requirement for a carrier-based attack aircraft with jet propulsion and with the ability to deliver nuclear weapons. The first prototype flew in October, 1952, and Skywarriors entered service in March, 1956. Douglas Aircraft Company produced 280 Skywarriors, including attack, photo-reconnaissance, electronic countermeasures, training, transport, and refueling tanker versions. The A3 was the largest and heaviest aircraft to operate from aircraft carriers. In the 1960s, the A3's role in nuclear deterrence faded, as the navy developed its ballistic missile submarines. By 1971, the Skywarriors still in service were employed primarily as tankers or in reconnaissance roles in Vietnam. The last Skywarriors were retired from active duty in September, 1991. Skywarriors first operated from *Lexington* as part of Air Group 21 during the ship's Western Pacific deployment of July 16 to December 19, 1958. With the exception of *Lexington*'s voyage around Cape Horn to join the Atlantic Fleet (July 23–September 11, 1962), A3s were aboard for every deployment of the ship prior to being reassigned as a training carrier in 1962.

PLATE A10: A4B AND TA-4 SKYHAWKS

Wingspan: 27 ft. 6 in.
Length: 40 ft. 3 3/4 in.
Height: 15 ft.
Weight: 24,500 lbs.
Power Plant: One 11,200-lb. thrust Pratt & Whitney J52-P-408A turbojet.
Armament: Two 20mm cannon; 8,200 lbs. of external ordnance.
Speed: 670 mph maximum.
Range: 2,055 miles.
Ceiling: 49,000 ft.
Manufacturer: McDonnell-Douglas Aircraft Company.

The Skyhawk was originally designed as a low-cost, "expendable" nuclear weapons delivery platform. It later became a primary conventional ordnance light attack aircraft. A low-wing monoplane with a modified delta wing, the prototype A-4 first flew on June 22, 1954, and delivery to operational squadrons began in October of 1956. By 1968, the plane equipped thirty navy and Marine Corps squadrons. Carrier-based pilots nicknamed the plane "Scooter" because of its nimble performance. The Skyhawk served the Blue Angels from 1974 to 1986, the longest of any aircraft flown by the navy's precision flight demonstration team. The A-4 at right is a single-seat fighter flown by Rear Adm. William "Bill" McGowen, who retired as commander of Naval Air Station Corpus Christi in 1993. McGowen's plane is similar to those operated off *Lexington* by squadron VA-144 of Air Group 14 during the ship's Western Pacific deployment from November 9, 1961, to May 12, 1962. The Skyhawk in the background is a two-seat trainer of the type operated from *Lexington* during the ship's training career, and it displays the traditional orange-and-white trainer paint scheme.

PLATE A11: F-4A PHANTOM II

Wingspan: 38 ft. 5 in.
Length: 58 ft. 4 in.
Height: 16 ft. 3 in.
Weight: 54,600 lbs.
Power Plant: Two
   10,900-lb. thrust
   General Electric J79-
   GE-8B or 8C turbojets.
Armament: 20mm
   multi-barrel cannon,
   internally or on
   external pod; Sparrow
   or Sidewinder air-to-
   air missiles; 16,000
   lbs. external ordnance
   on wing or centerline
   pylons.
Speed: 1,500 mph
   (Mach 2.27) maximum.
Range: 2,300 miles.
Ceiling: 62,000 ft.
Manufacturer:
   McDonnell-Douglas
   Aircraft Corporation.

Pilots called the twin-engine Phantom "brutishly ugly" but loved its exceptional performance—a top speed of 1,500 mph (Mach 2.27), and a climb rate of more than 28,000 feet per minute. Originally conceived as a carrier-based all-weather interceptor, the Phantom also performed well in the all-weather reconnaissance and high- and low-altitude attack roles. Despite its age—first deliveries were in February, 1960—Phantoms were still in service in 1991, flying electronic countermeasures sorties in "Wild Weasel" squadrons during the Persian Gulf War. More than five hundred Phantoms were built before final deliveries in March, 1979.

PLATE A12: T-28B TROJAN

Wingspan: 40 ft. 1 in.
Length: 33 ft.
Height: 12 ft. 8 in.
Weight: 8,500 lbs.
Power Plant: One
   1,425-hp Wright
   R-1820-86 engine.
Speed: 343 mph
   maximum, 310 mph
   cruising.
Range: 1,060 miles.
Ceiling: 35,500 ft.
Manufacturer: North
   American Aircraft
   Corporation.

The T-28 Trojan entered naval service in 1952 after a decision to standardize navy and air force training. The navy ordered 489 T-28Bs, equipped with engines delivering almost twice the horsepower of the Air Force T-28A. An additional 299 Trojans, T-28Cs, were ordered with arresting gear and used for carrier qualifications of flight students in intermediate training. The T-28 was a primary and intermediate training aircraft for the navy for more than thirty years. Trojans were a familiar sight on *Lexington*'s flight deck during the ship's training career.

PLATE A13: T-2C BUCKEYE

Wingspan: 38 ft. 2 in.
Length: 38 ft. 4 in.
Height: 14 ft. 10 in.
Weight: 13,179 lbs.
Power Plant: Two
2,950-lb. thrust
General Electric
J-85-GE-4 turbojets.
Armament: External
wing pods of guns,
100-lb. practice
bombs, cluster bombs,
rockets, or target
towing gear.
Speed: 522 mph
maximum.
Range: 909 miles.
Ceiling: 40,400 ft.
Manufacturer: North
American Rockwell
Aviation.

The Buckeye was developed in the late 1950s as a low-cost, multi-stage trainer for the navy. Straightforward and unspectacular, its designers relied on systems already proven in other aircraft produced by North American Rockwell, such as the FJ-1 Fury and the T-28 Trojan. The Buckeye was used at every level of flight training from initial to carrier qualification, including gunnery and bombing training. The original T-2A had a single engine, but later B and C models were powered by two turbojets. Like the Trojan, Buckeyes accounted for many of the nearly half a million arrested landings made on *Lexington*.

PLATE A14: T-34B MENTOR

Wingspan: 32 ft. 10 in.
Length: 25 ft. 11 in.
Weight: 3,000 lbs.
Power Plant: One
225-hp Continental
0-470-4 turboprop.
Speed: 188 mph
maximum.
Manufacturer: Beech
Aircraft Company.

The first T-34s purchased by the navy were T-34Bs, like this unit on board *Lexington*; they are piston-powered aircraft with modest performance. In the early 1970s, the B models were phased out in favor of the more powerful turboprop C version. The T-34C is the aircraft currently used by the navy for primary training of pilots and naval flight officers. It has served in that role since the mid-1970s. Until recently, the T-34B on board *Lexington* was used by the navy for recruitment.

Glossary

aft: Toward the rear of the ship.

afterburners: The devices located on the tailpipe of a jet engine that use hot exhaust gases to inject extra fuel into the exhaust system in order to increase thrust and speed.

air boss: Navy slang for the air officer of a carrier; often holds the rank of captain and is in charge of overall air operations on board the ship.

air group: The pilots, support personnel, and aircraft aboard a carrier at any time; it is designated CVG plus a group number. Groups include more than one squadron, and each squadron is assigned specific roles, such as air superiority (fighters) or attack (fighter-bombers and bombers).

AirOps: Shortened form of air operations.

amidships: In the middle of the ship.

anchor ring: The large metal loop at the end of the anchor shank (the straight stem of the anchor), to which the anchor chains are connected.

angled flight deck: An asymmetrical flight deck, the aft portion of which is angled to the port side several degrees off the centerline of the ship's keel. Angled flight decks provide a landing area on carriers that allow the pilot a second chance at landing if the first attempt is unsuccessful. As such, it made aircraft carriers viable in the jet age.

arrested landing: A successful landing, that is, one in which the incoming aircraft snags an arresting wire stretched across the flight deck, which brings the plane to a halt.

arresting gear: Includes the arresting wires that snag the aircraft, the purchase cable that allows runout on the wires, and the arresting engines, which provide tension on the wires and cables and provide resistance to the forward motion of the aircraft.

armored belt: A sheet of vertical steel plate several inches thick, the outer facing often further hardened by carbonizing, located within the ship's hull to protect the vital machinery spaces from shellfire damage.

athwartships: Across the ship, from side to side.

battleships: Heavily armored and armed warships that, during World War II, actually weighed more than aircraft carriers. They mounted the largest available naval guns, but despite large batteries of antiaircraft weapons, they proved very vulnerable to air attacks during World War II. The U.S. Navy's fast battleships often accompanied aircraft carriers to protect them with additional antiaircraft fire. Also called dreadnoughts.

battle stars: Awards to individual ships for participation in specific battles. *Lexington* earned eleven of twenty-two possible battle stars awarded for Pacific duty during World War II.

blisters: Also known as bulges, these are areas containing many void compartments that were built into the sides of carriers to improve the ship's stability and to accommodate the new, heavier, angled flight decks during postwar modernization. The void spaces are usually filled with fuel or water.

boilers: Operating in principle like giant teakettles, boilers produce the steam needed to drive a ship's engines.

boiler uptakes: The large tubes leading from each boiler to the ship's funnel. The uptakes carry the gaseous by-products of the boilers out of the ship's interior.

bolter: Navy slang for an aircraft that is "waved off" while attempting to land. On an angled flight deck, the plane can accelerate out of the landing pattern and make a second attempt.

bosun: Shortened form of boatswain, a warrant officer in the navy who is in charge of a specific area of the ship, like the anchors. The bosun also calls, or "pipes," the crew to duty with a whistle, which serves as his badge of rank.

bow: The front of a ship; its forward-most point.

bridge: The central command-and-control station on board a warship. Most of the captain's time at sea is spent here, the ship is steered from here, and orders for maneuvers or actions to be taken are issued from here. The *Lexington* has two bridges: the navigation bridge (just described) and a flag bridge, from which admirals could direct entire fleets of ships.

bridle: A very strong line that plays a key role in launching jet aircraft with a catapult. The bridle is attached to the aircraft's fuselage and to a towing shuttle on the catapult, and it transmits the high-velocity forward motion of the catapult to the aircraft, hurling the plane aloft at speeds of up to 125 miles per hour from a launch area only a few hundred feet long.

brig: The ship's jail.

bulkhead: The interior walls of a ship, subdividing its internal space into smaller compartments.

bullnose: Navy slang for the front end of a ship; with anchor hawse pipes on each side of the narrow, vertical bow line, it resembles a bull's nose.

captain's mast: A limited court of inquiry, used when the ship is at sea. Crewmen accused of infractions of navy regulations are brought before the captain's mast; the captain alone determines guilt or innocence and punishment.

CATCC: Acronym for Carrier Air Traffic Control Center, which controls both inbound and outbound traffic from the ship in much the same way an airport approach control radar facility does.

CCA: Acronym for Carrier Controlled Approach, when CATCC uses radar to guide planes to the ship during poor visibility.

centerline: In alignment with the ship's keel. Early carrier elevators were located in the center of the flight deck, and thus were centerline elevators.

CIC: Acronym for Combat Information Center, located during World War II on the gallery deck of the Lexington. The center processes information on both surface and air targets, directs the ship's own aircraft against attackers, and directs the fire of the ship's antiaircraft battery.

class: Any group of ships built to the same basic design characteristics. In the U.S. Navy, a class is named for the first ship in the group to have the keel laid. USS Essex was the first ship in the Essex class.

clock, 24-hour: Military time, which continues the numerical count past noon. Thus, 1 P.M. is 1300 hours, and midnight is 2400 hours. One minute past midnight is 0001 hours.

COD aircraft: Carrier Onboard Delivery aircraft, a utility plane used as a "fetch-and-tote" shuttle for the ship.

conn: Controlling the ship by issuing the orders that direct speed and course.

deck angle: That portion of the angled flight deck that is angled to port, away from the centerline. Lexington's deck angle is 520 feet long, while the complete angled flight deck is 910 feet long.

deck: The floor surface of a level within the ship that runs the complete length of the hull. A level that runs only part of the hull length is called a platform.

deck-edge elevators: Elevators located at the edge of the flight deck. This design has completely replaced centerline elevators on modern carriers.

department: All those people working in one area (e.g., the engine rooms and boiler rooms, called the engineering department).

dive-bomber: A type of aircraft employed extensively during World War II, it delivered its attack by going into a steep dive at the target, then pulling out of the dive at the moment it released its bomb load.

DRT: Acronym for Dead Reckoning Tracer, a navigation department instrument that automatically records all course and speed changes on paper as they occur.

ECM: Acronym for Electronic Countermeasures, a specialty that developed along with radar and other electronics. ECM specialists intercept enemy radar and/or electronic transmissions and either jam them, so that the results are unintelligible, or divert them to a decoy target.

escort carriers: The smallest carriers built by the Allied navies during World War II. Such ships rarely weighed as much as ten thousand tons, had very small air groups of twenty-five to thirty planes, and were used primarily to escort convoys and provide air cover against attacks by enemy aircraft or submarines.

executive officer: The second in command of a warship. Often called "the Ex-oh" (American), or "Number one" (British).

fantail: The open, aftermost area of a ship.

fathom: A nautical measure of depth, representing six feet.

fiddle bridge: Navy slang for a system of leafspring supports used to hold arresting wires some three inches above the flight deck, making them easier for aircraft to snag with the tailhook. Fiddle bridges are collapsible, so an aircraft will not snag more than one wire on a landing.

fighter-bomber: An attack aircraft that evolved late in World War II, which made use of the much higher speeds of fighter planes to deliver ordnance against surface targets. By the war's end, the fighter-bomber had almost completely displaced the dive-bomber and had reduced the torpedo bomber to a subordinate role.

flaps: Movable panels on the wings of aircraft, used to increase lift or decrease speed.

fleet carriers: Aircraft carriers sized to operate the largest possible air group. During World War II, such ships weighed at least twenty-five thousand tons and operated up to a hundred aircraft. The U.S. Navy operates only fleet carriers today.

flight deck: The flat, open upper deck of a carrier, from which aircraft are launched and on which they land.

flush-deck carriers: Early carriers built without any superstructure, or islands. Command-and-control stations were mounted along the edges of flight decks, sometimes in retractable compartments.

forward: Toward the front of the ship.

foul deck: A carrier's deck is "foul" when aircraft, equipment, personnel, or some problem prevents landing operations.

freeboard: The portion of a ship's hull from its upper deck to its waterline. Carriers had more freeboard than other warships.

full throttle: An aircraft is at full throttle when the pilot advances the fuel flow control to its maximum limit. Planes must be at full throttle for catapult launch.

funnel: The ship's smokestack.

gallery deck: The compartments located immediately below a carrier's flight deck and above the open hangar deck.

geedunk: Navy slang for sweets, like ice cream or pastries.

general quarters: The crew goes to general quarters when battle is anticipated.

gun directors: The targeting devices, optical or radar-controlled, that direct the ship's guns with maximum accuracy.

halyards: The rope lines from which signal flags send visual messages to other ships.

hangar deck: The large open space beneath a carrier's flight deck used to house and/or maintenance aircraft.

hawse pipe: The housing that pierces the forward part of the ship through the side of the hull, into which the shank of the anchor is drawn when the ship is under way.

holdback bar: An hourglass-shaped metal bar, used to restrain, or hold back, an aircraft just before it is launched by catapult. The bar attaches to the plane's after fuselage and to the catapult holdback unit. When the catapult fires, the bar breaks, releasing the plane. Holdback bars are of different strengths, depending on the size and weight of the aircraft.

hull number: In the U.S. Navy, each ship hull on which construction is begun receives an alphanumeric hull number. Lexington is CV-16, the sixteenth aircraft carrier hull laid down by the navy. The combinations of letters designate different types of ships, and hull numbers increase as more units are built.

hydraulics: Any system that makes use of liquids and the motion of liquids as a means of delivering power or movement.

island: Navy slang for the superstructure of an aircraft carrier. Carriers have very small superstructures in the midst of a "sea" of flight deck space, thus "islands."

JBD: Acronym for Jet Blast Deflector, a shield of water-cooled plates that lies flat on the flight deck until elevated behind an aircraft prior to a catapult launch, in order to protect personnel from afterburner injury.

kamikaze: "Divine wind" in Japanese, this was the name taken by Japanese suicide pilots who attempted to ram their planes into American warships in the late stages of World War II.

keel: A ship's spine; a huge beam that runs the length of the hull, on which the rest of the vessel's structure is built. Laying the keel is the first step in any ship construction.

knot: A nautical measure of speed, equivalent to 1.1516 miles per hour on land.

levels: The platforms above a ship's main, or first, deck. On aircraft carriers, the floor of the hangar deck is considered the main deck, so the first interior level of the superstructure is 01, the gallery deck is 02, the flight deck 03, and so on into the superstructure.

liberty: Navy slang for shore leave when a ship is in port.

light fleet carrier: The smaller carriers built by all combatants during World War II; the U.S. Navy used converted cruiser hulls. The ships weighed between ten thousand and fifteen thousand tons, and they had air groups smaller than those of fleet carriers but larger than those of escort carriers.

list: The slant or lean of a ship in relation to its vertical axis, usually after battle damage floods compartments on one side of the vessel.

LSO: Acronym for Landing Signals Officer, a naval aviator who is responsible for directing the final landing procedures of an aircraft. Carriers usually have an LSO for each type of aircraft in the air group.

meatball: Navy slang for the bright orange, vertically oriented light of the Optical Landing System, which gives pilots vertical orientation to the flight deck during landing approach.

mess: The areas on a ship where the crew takes its meals.

muzzle velocity: The speed at which a shell exits the gun barrel, expressed in feet per second.

navigation: The science of charting the course of a ship.

OOD: Acronym for Officer of the Deck, usually a highly qualified junior office in charge of conning the ship, under the direction of the captain or some other senior officer.

oxidation: The combining of oxygen with another substance. Aboard carriers, oxidation involving combustible fuels in the presence of an igniting agent was a major hazard, and separating combustibles from oxygen was a major responsibility of damage control teams.

plot: The area aboard a warship where navigation takes place, called the navigation plot, or where tactical plans are made for the ship or task force, called the tactical plot.

Pri-Fly: Shortened form of Priority Flight Control, an area in the superstructure from which flight operations are directed by the air officer.

psi: Acronym for pounds per square inch, the expression of the power of steam generated by the ship's boilers.

port: The left side of a ship when one faces the bow; it remains the port side when one faces the stern.

quad mount: A mount with four guns.

quarterdeck: Aboard modern warships, the entry point for officers and other dignitaries boarding the ship.

ready-use ammunition: The ammunition stored near the gun in which it will be used, usually "topside" in a carrier.

revolutions: Turns of the propeller.

rolling takeoffs: Carrier takeoffs in which catapults are not used.

Propeller-driven aircraft can make rolling takeoffs, but jets, because of their slow acceleration, cannot.

rpm: Acronym for revolutions per minute, an expression of the speed at which the ship's propellers are turning.

SCB: Acronym for Ship Characteristics Board, an organization within the navy that oversaw the reconstruction, redesign, and modernization of the fleet during the 1950s.

scout bomber: Archaic designation for aircraft intended to scout ahead of a task force. Scout work was assigned to the same type of aircraft used by dive-bombing squadrons, and by 1944 all scout functions had been merged with those of the dive-bombers.

shot: Navy slang for a catapult launch.

sponsons: The rounded cupolas and platforms that contained a carrier's antiaircraft guns. Usually mounted along the ship's sides, just below the flight deck, or on the sides of the island.

steam accumulators: The equipment used to "drag" steam off the boilers and transfer it to the catapult thrust units.

stability: The ability of a warship to list to one side without rolling over, sometimes called "turning turtle." Maintaining stability was crucial for warship survival, and ship design and damage control were oriented to that end.

starboard: Opposite of port; the right side of the ship when one faces the bow.

stanchions: Support columns in the interior of the ship.

stern: The rearmost point on a ship.

STS: Acronym for Special Treatment Steel, lighter than the carbon-hardened armor of battleships but capable of igniting aerial bombs before the bombs penetrate vital areas of the ship.

superstructure: The built-up area on a ship's upper deck, containing bridges, fire control areas, and other command-and-control stations.

task force: In World War II, the basic operational unit of the U.S. Navy in the Pacific. A task force contained several types of ships, including submarines, supply ships, and tankers for refueling at sea. The task force was usually built around several fleet carriers and was assigned a numerical designation, such as Task Force (TF) 58.

task group: A portion of a task force, performing a specific mission or specialty function. A task group might include carriers but could be composed only of battleships and escorts, for example. Task group designations included the task force number and a group number, as in Task Group 58.1.

topside weight: Weight carried high–at flight-deck level or above. A critical factor in carriers, which have more freeboard than other warship types and must therefore adhere to stricter stability requirements.

torpedo bomber: A carrier-based plane designed to attack surface ships with torpedoes. They carried a single torpedo slung beneath the plane, and they made their attacks a few feet above the water, maintaining as straight a course to the target as possible and launching the torpedo at the last minute. Casualties in torpedo squadrons were very high, especially early in the war.

trap: Navy slang for a successful arrested landing. Snagging the No. 3 arresting wire is a "perfect trap."

touch-and-go: The technique used by an aircraft "waved off" by the landing signals officer. The plane touches down on the deck angle briefly before powering away for another landing attempt. Naval aviators spent considerable practice time on touch-and-go as part of their carrier qualification training on Lexington.

voids: The compartments within the ship's hull that are purposely kept empty so they can be flooded to adjust the ship's trim or to correct a list following battle damage.

walkarounds: The catwalks on the outside of aircraft carrier hulls, below flight-deck level, used to facilitate movement without interfering with flight-deck operations.

watch: The on-duty period for naval personnel at their stations, stood in four-hour shifts unless the ship is at general quarters.

wave-off: A signal not to land given by the LSO when an aircraft's approach to the ship is incorrect for a safe, successful landing. The pilot goes around for another attempt.

Appendix A: Carrier *Lexington* (CV-16) in Profile

Builder: Bethlehem Steel (Fore River) Shipyard, Quincy, Massachusetts
Authorized: August 16, 1940
Keel Laid: September 15, 1941
Launched: September 26, 1942
Commissioned: February 17, 1943
Decommissioned: April 23, 1947
Recommissioned: August 15, 1955
Decommissioned: November 8, 1991

Displacement (design):	as built	in 1991
Standard tons	27,500	33,000*
Full load tons	36,380	42,000

Dimensions:		
Length overall	872 ft.	910 ft.
Length at waterline	820 ft.	no change (n/c)
Width (extreme)	147 ft. 6 in.	166 ft. 10 in.
Beam at waterline	93 ft.	103 ft.
Height (wl to flight deck)	52 ft.	n/c
Draft (full load)	28 ft. 6 in.	30 ft.

Machinery:		
Boilers	8 Babcock & Wilcox	n/c
Engines	4 Westinghouse steam turbines	n/c
Shafts	4	n/c
Propellers	16 ft. diameter	n/c

	as built	in 1991
Generators	4 turbo, 2 diesel	n/c
Fuel capacity (design)	6,330 tons	1.5 mil. gals.

Performance:

Boilers (design)	565 psi, 850°F	600 psi, 850°F
Shaft horsepower (design)	150,000	n/c
Speed (design)	33 kts	30 kts
Endurance	11,500nm/20kts	8,740nm-solidus 20kts
Generator capacity	5,500kW	7,000kW

Aeronautics:

Flight deck	862x108 ft.	910x142 ft.
Length of deck angle	not applicable (n/a)	520 ft.
Hangar deck	654x70 ft.	n/c
Hangar deck height	17.5 ft.	n/c
Aircraft	91	n/a
Elevators	2 centerline 1 deck-edge	1 deck-edge
Elevator lift capacity	28,000 lbs.	57,000 lbs.
Catapults	2 H4B hydraulic	2 C11 steam
Catapult launch area	96 ft.	211 ft.
Arresting gear	Mark IV	Mark VII
Aviation fuel capacity	231,650 gals.	400,000 gals.

Armament (design):

5-inch/38-caliber	12 (4x2, 4x1)	none
40mm antiaircraft	32 (8x4, Mark 4 mount)	none
20mm antiaircraft	44 (44x1)	none
.50-caliber Mark 31	24 (6x4 in 1955)	none

Protection:

Flight deck/gallery deck	none	n/c
Hangar deck	1.5 in.	n/c
Protective deck(s)	1.5 in.	n/c
Belt (508x10 ft.)	2.5–4 in.	none
Bulkheads	4 in.	n/c
Steering gear compt. (sides)	4 in.	n/c
Steering gear compt. (top)	2.5 in.	n/c
Pilothouse (sides)	1.5 in.	n/c
Pilothouse (top)	1 in.	n/c

Personnel:

Officers	268[+]	75[++]
Enlisted	2,363[+]	1,368[++]

---

[*] As modernized, 1955
[+] Includes air group personnel
[++] No permanent air group embarked

Appendix B:
Lexington's Commanding Officers

(Courtesy USS Lexington *Volunteer Organization)*

Capt. Felix B. Stump (February, 1943–April, 1944)
Capt. Ernest W. Litch (April, 1944–January, 1945)
Capt. Thomas H. Robbins (January, 1945–November, 1945)
Capt. Bradford E. Crow (November, 1945–October, 1946)
Lexington deactivates (October, 1946–April, 1947); into Pacific
   Reserve Fleet April, 1947; recommissions August, 1955.
Capt. Alexander S. Heyward, Jr. (August, 1955–October, 1956)
Capt. John W. Gannon (October, 1956–September, 1957)
Capt. Burl L. Bailey (September, 1957–July, 1958)
Capt. James R. Reedy (July, 1958–June, 1959)
Capt. Stanley E. Ruehlow (June, 1959–July, 1960)
Capt. Stockton B. Strong (July, 1960–July, 1961)
Capt. Hart D. Hilton (July, 1961–July, 1962)
Capt. Lucien C. Powell (July, 1962–July, 1963)
Capt. John M. Miller (July, 1963–June, 1964)
Capt. Quentin C. Crommelin (June, 1964–June, 1965)
Capt. Gordon A. Snyder (June, 1965–August, 1966)
Capt. Jack C. Heishman (August, 1966–August, 1967)
Capt. Edward W. Gendron (August, 1967–January, 1969)
Capt. Wayne E. Hammett (January, 1969–March, 1970)
Capt. Cyrus F. Fitton (March, 1970–April, 1971)
Capt. Jack E. Davis (April, 1971–December, 1972)
Capt. Charles C. Carter (December, 1972–August, 1973)
Capt. Jack E. Davis (August, 1973–November, 1973)*
Capt. Donald E. Moore (November, 1973–July, 1975)
Capt. Thornwell F. Rush (July, 1975–May, 1977)
Capt. Eugene B. McDaniel (May, 1977–November, 1978)

Capt. Phillip E. Johnson (November, 1978–June, 1980)
Capt. William H. Green, Jr. (June, 1980–December, 1981)
Capt. James W. Ryan (December, 1981–June, 1983)
Capt. Harold J. Bernsen (June, 1983–December, 1984)
Capt. Paul M. Feran (December, 1984–November, 1986)
Capt. Haywood G. Sprouse (November, 1986–May, 1988)
Capt. C. Flack Logan (May, 1988–December, 1990)
Capt. William Kennedy (December, 1990–November, 1991)

---

* Second tour of duty

Appendix C:
War Cruises of USS
Lexington (CV-16)

(Courtesy USS Lexington *Volunteer Organization)*

Shakedown Cruise: May 11, 1943–June 8, 1943–Caribbean Sea/Trinidad

Group/Squadron	Aircraft/Type
CVG-16/VF-16	F4F-4 Wildcat/fighter
CVG-16/VB-16	SBD-4 Dauntless/dive-bomber
CVG-16/VT-16	TBF-1 Avenger/torpedo bomber

Transit to Pearl Harbor—July 4, 1943–August 8, 1943

Group/Squadron	Aircraft/Type
CVG-16/VF-16	F6F-3 Hellcat/fighter
CVG-16/VB-16	SBD-5 Dauntless/dive-bomber
CVG-16/VT-16	TBF-1 Avenger/torpedo bomber

First War Cruise: September 11, 1943–December 9, 1943—Central Pacific

Group/Squadron	Aircraft/Type
CVG-16/VF-16	F6F-3 Hellcat/fighter
CVG-16/VB-16	SBD-5 Dauntless/dive-bomber
CVG-16/VT-16	TBF-1 Avenger/torpedo bomber

Dates	Location
September 18, 1943	Tarawa
October 5–6, 1943	Wake Island
November 19, 1943	Tarawa-Makin
December 4, 1943	Kwajalein

On December 4, *Lexington* was struck by a Japanese air-launched torpedo on the starboard side aft. The ship retired to Pearl Harbor for temporary repairs, then to Bremerton, Washington, for permanent repairs.

Second War Cruise (March 3, 1944–March 4, 1945)

MARCH 3, 1944–JULY 9, 1944—CENTRAL PACIFIC

Group/Squadron	Aircraft/Type
CVG-16/VF-16	F6F-3 Hellcat/fighter
CVG-16/VB-16	SBD-5 Dauntless/dive-bomber
CVG-16/VT-16	TBF-1C Avenger/torpedo bomber
CVG-16/VF(N)-76, Det. 3	F6F-3N Hellcat/night fighter

Dates	Location
March 18, 1944	Mille-Wotje
March 30, 1944	Palau
April 1, 1944	Woleai
April 21–25, 1944	Hollandia
April 28–30, 1944	Truk
May 1, 1944	Ponape
June 11–20, 1944	Saipan-Tinian
June 19–20, 1944	Japanese Fleet*
June 25, 1944	Guam
June 26, 1944	Pagan
July 2–5, 1944	Guam

JULY 14, 1944–NOVEMBER 9, 1944—CENTRAL/WESTERN PACIFIC

Group/Squadron	Aircraft/Type
CVG-19/VF-19	F6F-3/5/3N/3P/5N/5P Hellcat/fighter
CVG-19/VB-19	SB2C-3 Helldiver/dive-bomber
CVG-19/VT-19	TBM-1C Avenger/torpedo bomber
CVG-19/VF(N)-76, Det. 3	F6F-3N/TBM-1C/night fighters**

Dates	Location
July 18–21, 1944	Guam
July 26–27, 1944	Palau
August 5, 1944	Bonin Islands
September 6–7, 1944	Palau
September 9, 1944	Mindanao (Philippines)
September 12, 1944	Cebu-Leyte (Philippines)
September 14–18, 1944	Palau
September 22–23, 1944	Luzon (Philippines)
October 10, 1944	Nansei Shoto
October 13–14, 1944	Formosa
October 24–25, 1944	Japanese Fleet+
November 5–8, 1944	Manila (Philippines)

On November 5, *Lexington* sustained a hit on the starboard

side of the island by a Japanese kamikaze (suicide) plane. The ship retired to Ulithi Atoll for repairs.   side of the island by a Japanese kamikaze (suicide) plane. The side of the island by a Japanese kamikaze (suicide) plane. The   side of the island by a Japanese kamikaze (suicide) plane. The side of the island by a Japanese kamikaze (suicide) plane. The side of the island by a Japanese kamikaze (suicide) plane. The side of the island by a Japanese kamikaze (suicide) plane. The   147
ship retired to Ulithi Atoll for repairs.

DECEMBER 11, 1944–JANUARY 26, 1945—WESTERN PACIFIC

Group/Squadron	Aircraft/Type
CVG-20/VF-20	F6F-5/5N/5P Hellcat/fighter–night fighter
CVG-20/VB-20	SB2C-3 Helldiver/dive-bomber
CVG-20/VT-20	TBM-1C Avenger/torpedo bomber

Dates	Location
December 14–17, 1944	Luzon (Philippines)
January 3–5, 1945	Formosa
January 6–7, 1945	Luzon-Manila (Philippines)
January 9, 1945	Formosa
January 12, 1945	Indochina
January 15, 1945	Pescapore Islands
January 16, 1945	Hong Kong
January 21, 1945	Formosa
January 23, 1945	Nansei Shoto

FEBRUARY 10, 1945–MARCH 4, 1945—WESTERN PACIFIC

Group/Squadron	Aircraft/Type
CVG-9/VF-9	F6F-5/5N/5P Hellcat/fighter–night fighter
CVG-9/VBF-9	F6F-5/fighter-bomber
CVG-9/VB-9	SB2C-3/4 Helldiver/dive-bomber
CVG-9/VT-9	TBM-1C/torpedo bomber

Dates	Location
February 16–17, 1945	Tokyo
February 19, 1945	Iwo Jima
February 21–22, 1945	Iwo Jima
February 25, 1945	Tokyo
March 1, 1945	Nansei Shoto

Lexington returned to Ulithi on March 1 and sailed for the United States on March 7. The ship entered Puget Sound Navy Yard at Bremerton on March 31 and underwent routine overhaul during April and part of May.

Third War Cruise (June 13, 1945–December 15, 1945)

JUNE 13, 1945–SEPTEMBER 24, 1945—WESTERN PACIFIC

Group/Squadron	Aircraft/Type
CVG-94/VF-94	F6F-5/5N/5P Hellcat fighter–night fighter
CVG-94/VBF-94	F4U-4 Corsair/fighter-bomber
CVG-94/VB-94	SB2C-4E Helldiver/dive-bomber
CVG-94/VT-94	TBM-3E Avenger/torpedo bomber

148

Dates	Location
June, 1945	Leyte (Philippines)
	Wake Island
June 26, 1945	San Pedro Bay (Philippines)
July 10, 1945	Tokyo
July 15, 1945	Kamaishi (Japan)
	Hokkaido (Japan)
July 16, 1945	Tokyo
July 18, 1945	Yokosuka (Japan)
July 24, 1945	Kobe (Japan)
	Kure Naval Base (Japan)
July 28, 1945	Kure Naval Base
	Nagoya (Japan)
August 9, 1945	Honshu (Japan)
August 13, 1945	Tokyo
August 14, 1945	Hyakurigahara (Japan)
August 15, 1945	Japanese surrender announced
August 25, 1945	Patrols off Honshu
September 5, 1945	Tokyo Bay++
September 10, 1945	Tokyo Bay
September 15, 1945	Patrols off Honshu

SEPTEMBER 24, 1945–DECEMBER 15, 1945—WESTERN PACIFIC

Group/Squadron	Aircraft/Type
CVG-92/VF-92	F6F-5/5P Hellcat/fighter
CVG-92/VBF-92	F4U-1D/4 Corsair/fighter-bomber
CVG-92/VB-92	SB2C-4 Helldiver/dive-bomber
CVG-92/VT-92	TBM-3/3E Avenger/torpedo bomber

Dates	Location
September 24, 1945	Patrols off Japan
December 3, 1945	Sails for United States
December 16, 1945	San Francisco

Damage Inflicted on Enemy by *Lexington*

Aircraft destroyed by ship's guns	17
Aircraft shot down by air groups	387
Aircraft destroyed on the ground	635
Naval tonnage sunk or damaged	588,000
Merchant tonnage sunk or damaged	497,000

---

* First Battle of the Philippine Sea, the Marianas Turkey Shoot
** On board July 14, 1944, to October 1, 1944
+ Battle of Leyte Gulf
++ *Lexington* was the first U.S. fleet carrier to enter Tokyo Bay at the end of World War II

Suggested Further Reading

GENERAL

Dull, Paul S. *A Battle History of the Imperial Japanese Navy (1941–1945)*. Annapolis, Md.: Naval Institute Press, 1978. The author is American, but the perspective is largely Japanese in this balanced view of the naval war in the Pacific.

Keegan, John. *The Price of Admiralty: The Evolution of Naval Warfare*. New York: Penguin Books, 1988. A succinct essay on the coming of the aircraft carrier and a brilliant dissection of its most decisive moment—at Midway.

Macintyre, Donald. *The Naval War against Hitler*. New York: Charles Scribner's Sons, 1971. Important insights into the role of the aircraft carrier in the Mediterranean and against the U-boats.

Maclean, Anne, and Suzanne Poole, eds. *Fighting Ships of World Wars One and Two*. New York: Crescent Books, 1976. Excellent illustrations work well with concise text to describe the complicated carrier battles of World War II.

Morison, Samuel Eliot. *The Two-Ocean War*. Boston: Little, Brown, 1963. Admiral Morison does the impossible, collapsing his mammoth fourteen-volume *History of United States Naval Operations in World War II* into one volume—and making it work.

Prange, Gordon W. *At Dawn We Slept: The Untold Story of Pearl Harbor*. New York: Penguin Books, 1981. The most detailed analysis of the Japanese attack on Pearl Harbor, the moment carrier aviation came of age.

———. *Miracle at Midway*. New York: Penguin Books, 1982. Explores both sides of events surrounding the most important five minutes in American military history, when the war in the Pacific changed course 180 degrees.

Reynolds, Clark G. *The Fast Carriers: The Forging of an Air Navy*. Annapolis, Md.: Naval Institute Press, 1968. The men, the tactics—and the politics—that made the aircraft carrier the new capital ship of World War II.

Wilson, George C. *Supercarrier*. New York: Macmillan Publishing, 1986. A look inside the modern behemoths of the carrier force and the men who run them.

Chesneau, Roger. *Aircraft Carriers of the World: 1914 to the Present.* Annapolis, Md.: Naval Institute Press, 1984. Invaluable overview of every carrier type ever deployed by the world's navies.

Friedman, Norman. *U.S. Aircraft Carriers: A Design History.* Annapolis, Md.: Naval Institute Press, 1983. A comprehensive and very readable look at U.S. aircraft carrier design.

Lyon, Hugh. *The Encyclopedia of the World's Warships.* New York: Crescent Books, 1978. Good statistics, readable text, and drawings that are particularly useful in understanding aircraft carrier layout.

Raven, Alan. *Essex-Class Carriers.* Annapolis, Md.: Naval Institute Press, 1988. Concise text and extensive drawings bring to life the U.S. Navy's most successful carrier design.

Whipple, Judith, ed., and the USS *Lexington* Volunteer Organization. *USS Lexington: "The Blue Ghost" (AVT-16).* Corpus Christi: USS *Lexington* Museum on the Bay, 1993. Concise overview and good details on the cruises of this longest-serving of U.S. aircraft carriers.

Index

154